Wooden Spoon Society

RUGBY WORLD '97

EDITED BY

Nigel Starmer-Smith
and Ian Robertson

Queen Anne Press

A QUEEN ANNE PRESS BOOK

First published in 1996 by
Queen Anne Press, a division of
Lennard Associates Limited
Mackerye End
Harpenden, Herts AL5 5DR

A catalogue entry is available from the British Library

ISBN 1 85291 574 9 (paperback)
ISBN 1 85291 580 3 (hardback)

Production Editor: Chris Hawkes
Cover Design/Design Consultant: Paul Cooper
Reproduction: CMYK Graphics
Printed and bound in Slovenia

The publishers would like to thank Colin Elsey of Colorsport for
providing most of the photographs for this book.

Thanks to David Gibson of Fotosport, Sportsfile, Andrew Varley,
E & B Productions, Russell Cheyne and Allsport (UK) for additional
material.

Thanks also to Tony Williams for allowing the use of statistics and
fixtures prepared originally for the *Official Rugby Union Club Directory*
and to the *Daily Express* for permission to reproduce Bob McKenzie's
artice on the 1971 Lions reunion.

Finally many thanks to Heineken for their overall sponsorship
and to Cathay Pacific, Hongkong Bank, Next, Save & Prosper,
Cellnet, Coopers & Lybrand, Kenwood, Nokia, Pilkington, Sanyo,
Trocadero and Vauxhall for supporting this year's edition of the
Wooden Spoon Society Rugby World '97.

CONTENTS

WOODEN SPOON SOCIETY
– the Charity of British Rugby

It is not often given to a charity to be able to publish its own book. Not just a book for the dedicated and committed membership but a book that has become an established favourite among the rugby fraternity.

We are therefore deeply grateful for the generous support of Whitbread – through Heineken – for making this book, the *Wooden Spoon Society Rugby World*, possible. We are further indebted to all the other advertisers, please read their copy and purchase their wares.

Thanks also to the co-editors, Nigel Starmer-Smith and Ian Robertson, for allowing the full flower of their penhood and their collective stream of literary inspiration to reflect the interest and contribute to the financial wherewithal of the Wooden Spoon Society.

It is less than 14 years since five rather dispirited Englishmen, clutching a wooden spoon following England's third defeat in that Home International season, surveyed a rather bleak future in a Dublin bar and said: 'What future?' With the benefit of foresight, they could have said: 'What a future!'

In the intervening years a charity was conceived, went through the pangs of birth and development, and has emerged in full flower with its own yearbook within the sport that gave it life.

Remarkable progress, almost precocious in its performance, but given stability and depth by the overwhelming support and quality of its membership.

We trust you will enjoy this book ; it has a long tradition for excellence thanks to the constant stewardship of Whitbread who have lent their name and reputation for the past eight years.

We salute you Whitbread, for the reputation you have created, and standards you have set. Wooden Spoon Society will be proud to do justice to your bequest and improve, where possible, upon your performance.

If you are now asking, how can I be part of Wooden Spoon? The answer is an easy one, come and join us!

Details from: The Spoon Office, 81 Middle Wall, Whitstable, Kent CT5 1BW
Tel: 01227 772295 Fax: 01227 772296

A YEAR IN THE LIFE OF SPOON

BY **DAVID ROBERTS**

As an event-organizing charity we tend to meet fairly often; have fun on a frequent basis; and raise loads of money very regularly!

The Bracknell RFC raffle raises on average £5000 each year for Spoon.

1995-96 has been a fairly typical Spoon year.

We re-united the victorious '71 British Lions to New Zealand over four days and four events – a Stag Dinner in Cardiff, a Lions-Am Golf Day at Celtic Manor GC, a Gala Dinner in London and a day at the Middlesex Sevens at Twickenham

Front row, Chris Rea, John Dawes and Aly Biggar, all '71 Lions; at the back (l to r), BBC's Ian Robertson, Spoon Director David Roberts, Spoon Chairman David Hammond and Kelvin Byron and Keith Pritchard, of sponsors Basildon Chemicals plc, at the East India Club.

The Spoon roundel goes up at Twickenham.

Peter Winterbottom talks to Twickenham Spoon Terrace regular, Helen Smith at the 'W' party.

The Scottish Committee welcome the Princess Royal to Murrayfield.

And talking of international rugby, this year saw the opening of the second Wooden Spoon Bar at Twickenham and also the fixing of the Spoon logo which proudly overlooks the ground.

We also enjoyed our annual 'W' party for the wheelchair Spooners at Twickenham. An event much appreciated by our chairbound members and attended by the great and good of 'Twickers' including HRH the Prince Edward.

Another royal event in 1995 saw the opening by HRH the Princess Royal of our Wooden Spoon Wheelchair Terrace at Murrayfield.

We welcomed two international teams and both did great tribute to their Wooden Spoon Society rugby colours. The first team to hit these shores were the Ithubans

The Ithubans parade their Spoon colours.

from Cape Town, South Africa, the guest side at the Middlesex Sevens at Twickenham. Throughout their tour the Ithubans proudly wore their Spoon rugby shirts.

Later in the year, July to be precise, we had the return of our all-conquering Spoon Fijians. The venue was Abertillery in South Wales and they were the star guest side along with other teams drawn from the world over for the first playing of the International Sevens Wales '95. It was too easy for the gifted Fijians, led by Waiseli Serevi, and so Wooden Spoon coloures featured in yet another sevens tournament victory.

The Fijians at Abertillery.

Thanks to our friends at Stourbridge Rugby Football Club (and in particular IRFB member and Stourbridge stalwart John Jeavons-Fellows) a grand selection of top Midlands sides competed

Proud Northampton skipper David Merlin receives the Spoon Crystal Trophy from Midlands Chairman Ron Sutton whilst Tournament organiser Richard Connett looks on.

ferociously for the Spoon Crystal Trophy in the Midlands Tens tournament. The eventual winners were a strong Northampton who won a closely-fought final.

Willie John McBride and Jerry Guscott modelled the new Spoon town tie for us when it was launched in 1996.

Immediate past Lions and Scotland captain, Gavin Hastings, was captain again when he led the Lions Four Peaks team, including Mike Griffiths (Wales) and Gareth Chilcott (England), up the four highest mountains of Scotland, England, Wales and Ireland, helping to raise over £220,000 for Wooden Spoon from the Challenge.

Can you believe that a man who, non-stop, has just climbed 15,000 feet, walked 35 miles and driven 1900 miles, all in under 48 hours can look this cheerful?
Far left Willie John McBride and Jerry Guscott in their new Spoon town ties.

ALWAYS ONE TO SPOT A GOOD OPENING, ONCE ARCHIE HEARD ABOUT SAVE & PROSPER UNIT TRUSTS, THERE WAS NO STOPPING HIM

If you'd like to hear more about Save & Prosper Unit Trusts, just ring us on our free Moneyline: 0800 829 100. It could be just the break you need.

© RFU 1990

SAVE & PROSPER

THE INVESTMENT HOUSE
SPONSORS OF ENGLISH RUGBY

COMMENT

SCANT TIME TO REFLECT

BY **BILL BISHOP** OBE

When asked by Nigel Starmer-Smith to provide a brief contribution to this *Wooden Spoon Society Rugby World*, I had a week or so to go to the AGM of the RFU, the day on which my term as President of the RFU would end.

I was hopeful that the turbulent year would be brought to a conclusion in relative calm – with my experience, I should have known better. Having weathered the major part of the storm that the International Rugby Football Board's decision in Paris last August caused throughout the game, and with all the English clubs now under the umbrella of the RFU, was it too much to hope at last for calmer waters? There was still hope that the decision by the RFU to negotiate its own television contract, an intention that had been known for some time, would be accepted by the other three home unions – after discussion, and no doubt with some concession.

For a while this did not seem to be the case and, although the existing contract with the BBC had one more season to run, England were threatened with expulsion from the Five Nations Championship.

Why did this happened? Why was it allowed to happen? What were the RFU doing? There were many reasons why, but the fundamental reason and the one responsible for so many of the problems in the new 'open/professional game' was the decision by the IRFB to totally rescind or abolish the amateur regulations which had underpinned the game for 100 years.

For Bill Bishop his tenure as President of the RFU coincided with the most difficult year that the game of rugby had had to face.

Last year's officers and committee were faced with unprecedented problems, with no set of rules and little guidance from the International Board. The southern hemisphere were in close season, we were just starting; so the RFU declared a moratorium for the season 1995–96 to give some breathing space. Players at all levels were worried, but particularly at the top level, so an international squad contract for the 1995–96 England squad was produced, this was followed by the RFU model club/player contract issued to all clubs in May 1996.

Most of those involved in the game, those who play, administer or support, are concerned about the future, the stable, traditional game is gone forever; what will now happen to the new open game? One thing is certain, there is no going back. Rugby union will never be the same game again and it is the affect on the people in the game that concerns me most.

Already there are signs of instability, with money pouring into a few selected clubs and the resultant transfers of international and rugby league players.

The 1996–97 season is going to be very interesting in so many ways, not least the results and final placing of the clubs in divisions one and two. Will some clubs be able to buy success, I imagine so in may cases. What I cannot envisage is the same playing squad containing both full time professional rugby players and those with other careers.

One thing is certain, the days of the traditional committee man at the top level are numbered. A club will be run by a board of directors, certainly an EPRUC club in divisions one and two.

Although there is a clean cut-off point between divisions two and three, this will not be where professionalism finishes. The question is how far down will it go? The choice is there for each club at whatever level. If money is available any club can decide to pay its players.

The RFU fought hard to retain overall control of rugby in England and this has been achieved, the other important principle was that the open game was 'seamless'. Players and clubs alike are free to adapt their degree of professional commitment to the game according to ambition, ability and financial standing.

In its 125th year, the game will embark on its first professional season. It was inevitable that this would happen and that we would follow the route taken in the southern hemisphere and accelerated by the World Cup. The simple fact is that the national squad wanted payment for playing and a package, whereby the England squad players would receive payment for promoting the game, was agreed before the party left for South Africa. This was subsequently converted to the international squad contract.

As to the future, we may look at the experience of rugby league, but rugby union is different in that it covers the whole of the country and is numerically so much larger. As we are not a major spectator sport at club level, gates can only provide a small percentage of money needed, so there is no real comparison to English football.

TV and sponsorship in various forms will provide the main sources of income and will no doubt have a large say in the running of the clubs/companies. What must be avoided, and I know there is agreement on this issue, is clashes between clubs and country over the release of players, and this is further complicated by the number of other home union players in the national league.

It will be a difficult season. The game will take a while to settle but, if we are to retain what is best in our great game, some flexibility, understanding and give-and-take by all parties will be needed. I wish my successor, John Richardson, all good wishes for the task he has taken on. Much remains to be done, but he can build on the many achievements of last season when a lot of ground work was put in by a lot of people.

My year as President was a difficult one, but hugely rewarding in a lot of ways and certainly not to be forgotten. I only hope that the England team that I was fortunate to preside over, and who won the Five Nations Championship, have a chance to defend their title.

performance from

NEXT

A GAME IN CHAOS – is professionalism worth it?

BY **JOHN REASON**

Until a year ago, rugby union football had prospered so much in the last hundred years that it had grown into one of the great success stories of world sport – as an amateur sport.

Apart from the unique structure and fascination of the game itself, amateurism was the staple of its existence. Indeed, it was probably *the* most significant factor which led to the remarkable development of the game, because of the socially broadening effect it had on its playing base.

This enabled a digger driver like Ray Prosser, of Pontypool and Wales, to become a friend for life of an international business tycoon as big as Tony O'Reilly and of upper-crust types like England's David Marques and John Young.

The lads and the lords found, to their delight, that they could play and laugh together, and knock seven bells out of each other, and so enjoy the experience that the memories and the comradeship would last for life.

The unique and quite different physical requirements for no fewer than twelve of the fifteen positions in a rugby team meant that any boy or man, no matter how different their shape of size, weight, height, strength or speed could play and enjoy rugby union at some sort of level.

And because it was an amateur game, a man of the soil could find himself playing alongside or against, and enjoying the company of a man of the cloth or a man of high finance or an eminence from the legal, medical or business professions.

It was a glorious fluke of sporting evolution. However, whilst the game was spreading worldwide, there were those who broke away and formed the Rugby League – because they wanted to be paid for playing. This never spread far beyond two northern counties in England, Lancashire and Yorkshire, and the eastern seaboard of Australia. It never caught on, as Rugby Union did, and in the end, after almost exactly 100 years, it was failing, and failing fast.

And all because the very first commandment in the International Rugby Football Board's very own bible defining the laws of the game stated that (and the statement was in tablets brought down from the mountain): 'The Game is an Amateur Game. No person is allowed, directly or indirectly to receive payment, benefit or other material reward, for taking part.'

Nothing could have been more specific.

Yet in the summer and autumn of 1995, the International Board held two fateful meetings, one in Paris, and the other in Tokyo. At those meetings, the Board managed to push the requirement of amateurism overboard without doing anything so sordid as actually having a vote on the subject.

This must rank as one of the most astonishing pieces of procedural manipulation in sporting history, particularly as England's two representatives on the International Board, John Jeavons-Fellows and Peter Brook, had been mandated to oppose payment to players for actually playing the game.

If they had fulfilled their mandate, and insisted upon a vote, and if they had given the lead which England had always provided since the days when England alone controlled the International Board, a threequarters voting majority would have been necessary to abandon amateurism. Fifteen votes out of twenty. That was unattainable.

But no vote was taken, and somehow or other, the member countries were allowed, in effect, to go off and do as they liked. Even Ronnie Dawson was shaking his head in sheer disbelief about this, and no one has seen more of the executive function of Rugby Union football worldwide than he has; captain of Ireland; captain of the 1959 British Lions; coach of the 1968 British Lions; member of the International Board; Chairman of the International Board; President of the Irish Rugby Union – the lot.

'How could the Board not take a vote on the most important clause.'

Apparently, South Africa wanted to acknowledge that the game in their country was covertly professional. Wales and France wanted to do the same, even though any lawyer could have told them that opting for the overt, rather than tolerating the covert, meant that Rugby's governing bodies would no longer be able to control player movement within the game. Acknowledgement of professionalism carries with it all the destructive and intrusive legislation relating to restraint of trade.

This meant that France would not be able to retain the draconian license system to stop player-poaching which they had found so necessary and had built up over sixty years – neither would anyone else. A player market would be established instantly, and it would be a chaotic free-for-all, or rather, a very expensive free-for-all; a market that would be dominated by money, rather than

Professionalism has brought with it a new breed – the moneyed club owner like Sir John Hall who has spread his interests to Newcastle Gosforth.

club loyalty; a market that would involve transfer fees, players' contracts, player-poaching and the rest; all utterly divisive for the member clubs of any union.

Australia and New Zealand, for their part, were terrified that they would lose key players to Rugby League, and even though Rugby League, anywhere in the world, had about as much future as John Cleese's celebrated Norwegian Blue parrot, those two countries could not see that the dive into professionalism would be the dive of the lemmings.

The implications for rugby in the Pacific islands are disastrous. Fiji, Tonga and Western Samoa bulge with natural playing talent, but because of the 'little brother' economics of the islands, it is inevitable that Australia and New Zealand will strip them bare.

The fitness requirements of professionalism will also change the social structure of the game worldwide. Men with university degrees and careers will simply not be able to participate in full-time training. So the playing communities will be increasingly drawn from the immigrant ghettos.

It would be difficult to imagine anything more catastrophic for the image and well-being of rugby football, because in terms of injury, and realistic career expectations, rugby is far too dangerous and short-lived a game to be viable as a job of work.

Another factor in the revolution and perhaps the most significant, was the potential income from satellite television. Any game which makes itself a pawn to television digs its own grave, but a significant number of players, and all too many of the game's administrators, could not wait to pick up their spades. Various entrepreneurs started talking telephone numbers to them, and began projecting mega-buck competitions which would span the globe and keep them in luxury for the rest of their lives. So the players began talking of nothing other than 'new money' and threatened breakaway movements. Instead of smiling quietly and letting them go, perhaps even giving the players a few bikes, the unions began to shiver. Small men do.

As if all this was not enough, there was one other consideration which probably had a bearing on the bedlam. This was the 1999 Rugby World Cup, to be held in Wales, and therefore, a projection very dear to the hearts of the Welsh.

It just so happened that the Chairman of the International Board at their meeting in Tokyo was Vernon Pugh, himself of Wales, and a lawyer as well, so the avoidance of any possible threat to the 1999 World Cup was a substantial interest to declare.

Very few people are in any doubt that if a vote had been taken in Tokyo, as it should have been, and amateurism had been retained, the southern hemisphere countries would have left the International Board. So there would have been no World Cup in Wales in 1999.

That might have been the greatest blessing that could be bestowed on the game, because the World Cup adds enormously to the pressure on players, and it is now clear that it only reveals, and even increases, the disparity between the haves and have-nots of international rugby.

Rugby is fast losing its sense of occasion, especially in the southern hemisphere. We are already seeing the law of diminishing returns coming into force.

As if all that was not enough, the Rugby Union in England then decided to

A game in flux. Rob Norster, Richard Moon and Peter Winterbottom at the Press Conference to launch the Rugby Union Players' Association. Now the players had to look after their own interests.

ditch eighty-five per cent of their television audience, and jeopardise the Five Nations Championship by going off on their own and negotiating a five-year satellite television contract independent of the other three Home Unions.

Even members of the Rugby Union committees were unhappy about this.

They knew it was a hideous mistake to treat Scotland, Ireland and Wales like second-class citizens, and because the committee were not allowed to see the contract, and discuss it, they had the gravest reservations about everything to do with it.

'Why the secrecy,' asked one, who is himself a very successful business man. He shook his head. 'There were all sorts of hidden agendas round that table,' he said.

As a result, an increasing number of England's clubs and constituent bodies are after the blood of the Rugby Union's officers and executive committee. The English game is facing civil war.

Is professionalism worth all that? Surely not.

PANDORA'S BOX

BY CLEM THOMAS

When Epimetheus opened the box given to Pandora by Zeus, all the evils flew out to inflict the world. Rugby followers are beginning to believe that the International Rugby Board have imposed a similar disaster by declaring the game open in October 1995, with not a single guideline to the countless voluntary and amateur administrators of what to expect in a professional game. But then, they had obviously not thought it through themselves!

As a result, we have seen the unedifying spectacle of the national unions and clubs of England and Wales falling out and threatening each other, before finally settling on an uneasy truce. Meanwhile, the Rugby Union started a war on two fronts, when, without reference to the other elected members of the committee or to the other home unions, they secretly negotiated a deal with Rupert Murdoch's Sky television, for a tournament which did not belong to them, thus breaking faith and friendship with the Celtic nations for the first time since the championship began, without France, in 1883.

This action was seen as high-handed duplicity and greed by the Celts and it created a frightening game of poker, as the other home unions using the Five Nations tournament as the stake threw England out of the championship. Sanity prevailed and the meeting of 23 July 1996 at Cardiff re-opened negotiations. It is, of course, unthinkable to have a tournament without England, the most historic dear enemy for all Celts.

At club level, it appears that all the old values have gone for good, as the Victorian style members' clubs disappear, to become limited companies and begin to move towards a typical corporate structure, with control passing from the democratic vote by members to a new structure of direction by an executive board, which can more readily respond to the pace of modern business and make rapid and meaningful decisions.

The members' interests are less likely to be protected in a private company than they are in a public limited liability company. In the latter, they can take a stake and vote and, under company law, the directors have to act in the interests of all the shareholders.

Last year the members owned the clubs. Some still do, but in the new ethos that is impractical and it is important to examine what structure the clubs put in place. The financial risks of not being a limited company are far too great and only the foolish or the mega-rich would undertake the role of trustee or guarantor; so, we must move away from being members' clubs because it would be too dangerous.

The professional era will now be dominated by the profit motive, because a club must, from now on, produce a positive cash flow if it is to prosper and be able to fund new investment and development. It is no longer a question of the Treasurer balancing the books as they did in the old days, with the simple equation of **income = expenditure**; now it must be **income - expenditure = profit**, which is a quite different philosophy. Running a club as a business will require distinctive and more complex management skills. A club will need to build up assets which will now include the players, against which they will raise money, with the repayments met out of the club's cash flow.

There are three major sources for generating revenue and cash flow; there is the traditional membership and gates' receipts, merchandising and sponsorship, but most important of all are television receipts, a source which has never before been accessed, as previously it was controlled by the rugby unions. This is where the current power struggle is taking place between clubs and unions. Latterly, the clubs received something like £10,000 from television, but from next season it will be measured in hundreds of thousands of pounds. The first division Welsh clubs, back in July, negotiated £22,500,000 for a five-year contract with Sky, which would give each club some £400,000 per annum.

At the national level, the Welsh, Irish and Scots took a big risk in rejecting the deal with Sky, because they may have blocked a substantial income in order to ensure the principle that rugby will be seen by the majority and not the few. Propagation of the game is hugely important, so here is an example where the commercial interest can be outweighed by the common good.

The conflict of interest between clubs and the unions will continue and, now that they are profit- or loss-making entrepreneurs, the clubs will increasingly be crossing swords with the game's governing bodies. In the end, the clubs should win, just as football's Premier League has done by controlling its own television and merchandising revenues. The future must lay in the clubs managing their own television revenue and the unions must be happy with the television take

Philippe Sella succumbs to the lure of money. He will be joined at Nigel Wray-backed Saracens next year by former Australia fly half Michael Lynagh.

from the Five Nations. This is also the anwer to England's requirements for more money because they have the bigger parish to administer.

Inevitably, a new élite will emerge, and they will be the wealthier and better organised clubs. It will be survival of the fittest and they will become like football's super clubs, with teams being owned by wealthy individuals and companies, with the franchises bought and sold. We have already had a taste of this with Sir John Hall acquiring Newcastle, Ashley Levett financing Richmond, and Peter Thomas controlling Cardiff, to mention but a few.

Television ratings and revenues will be of major importance as rugby moves from being merely a sport to a product to be marketed and exploited and, therefore, the game will be manipulated to become more attractive to the spectator. No longer is it going to be a game for the players, who in the past were asked or invited to play; instead they will be told to play in a certain way and they will be penalised, even fined, for not reaching required standards of fitness and performance.

Richmond's new signings. From left to right: Ben Clarke (Bath), Scott Quinnell (Wigan RLFC), Jim Fallon (Leeds RLFC), Richard West (Gloucester), Adrian Davies (Cardiff), Andy Moore (Cardiff) and Darren Crompton (Bath).

The reason why television has recently been chasing rugby is because it has a high percentage of A, B1 and B2 audiences, as ITV discovered when they secured the television contract for the last two World Cups.

The danger may be that the new master, television, will demand law changes, which will alter the character of the game. Rugby supporters will resent any over-emphasis on making the game a spectacle with Harlem Globetrotter-style performances, which are more show business than reality. Already, law changes and tampering with the scoring values and the introduction of bonus points are seeing freaky, one-sided, high scores, as the whole effort goes into all-out attack, while organised defence is neglected.

The southern hemisphere Super 12 competition, which has been a huge financial and popular success, was marked by excessively high scores, as were the results of the Heineken League in Wales last season. This is what can happen if you tinker with the scoring values. You could also discern the difference in attitude between the Tri-Nations southern hemisphere tournament and the Super 12 competition.

Another great danger is that clubs, encouraged by their new riches, will go on a spending spree which they cannot afford. Prudence will surely be the name of the game in the early years of professionalism, for buying 'star' players is not a guarantee to success. Cardiff, who are probably the richest club in Wales, failed to win the league or cup last season, in spite of acquisitions, and were pipped at the post by the far less fashionable, but more gnarled, Neath and Pontypridd.

The transfer market is going to be full of pitfalls and there will be huge risks involved, and therefore, clubs will have to invest more in their junior teams, not only because they may have a low asset base, but because this will be a way to build up assets by the judicious buying and selling of players. One can reflect that Manchester United were one of the lowest spenders on players in the Premier League last season, yet achieved huge success.

Transfer deals will be a major factor in the profitability of the clubs and some clubs, who have a first-class young player-development scheme, will become assett rich, while others will be forced to take huge risks in the transfer market. Player contracts and insurance will have to be watertight.

It must also be remembered that the top English and Welsh clubs, like Cardiff or Bath, do not compete in financial terms with teams like Manchester United or Tottenham Hotspur. You simply have to compare the viewing figures of *Match of the Day* and *Rugby Special* to see there is no comparison.

From now on, each first division rugby club will require between £700,000 and £1,000,000 per annum if it is to pay its players and function properly, which is enough to make the old fashioned Club Treasurer rush off to the nearest cardiac department.

As I say, it is going to be a different world, where some will succeed and others will fail, which is the way of all commerce. In the early days, caution and prudence will be required, but then there is also the argument of 'who dares, wins'. As to the game itself, well it is bound to change, and I must confess that I am beginning to wonder what game the educated middle-class are going to adopt from now on, as secondary schoolboys become torn between giving time to what is becoming a very hard game, or building a future career.

AURI SACRA FAMES

BY **PAUL STEPHENS**

One of the prized certainties in the 125-year existence of the Rugby Football Union was that those who worked for its future not only had the best interests of the game at heart, but were sure of the way ahead. In the 125 days which preceded the start of the 1996–97 season, the cherished notion that the game in England was still in safe hands became just another piece of sporting make-believe.

The signs that all was not well within the body of the union were evident during the last weeks of the previous season, culminating in the Wigan rugby league team's victory at the Middlesex Sevens and the two, historic cross-code matches between Bath and Wigan.

As the last joints were being sealed to complete the rebuilding of the towering Twickenham grandstands, cracks were beginning to appear with alarming frequency within the administration, eventually leading to an unprecedented outbreak of bickering and antagonism. Confidence in the newly-appointed Secretary Tony Hallett, plummeted, while the Executive Committee, under their tenderfoot Chairman Cliff Brittle, soon lost all credibility with a succession of extraordinary decisions, as they lurched from crisis to crisis. With a stadium the envy of the world, the RFU was becoming the laughing stock of the global game.

By failing to respond proactively after the International Rugby Football Board legitimised payments to players at their Paris meeting in August 1995, the RFU left themselves vulnerable to the claims of all manner of special interest groups, some of whom within months were threatening the very fabric of the English game, if not the RFU itself. The most vocal of these was the newly-formed English Professional Rugby Union Clubs, who broke away from the National Clubs' Association to form a limited company representing the Courage League Division One and Two clubs.

Well before EPRUC's Chairman Donald Kerr mischievously threatened to lead his member clubs in a breakaway from the union if their demands were not met, the RFU staged a Special General Meeting at the Birmingham Convention Centre. Present were some 800 delegates from England's rank-and-file clubs who were balloted to decide if John Jeavons-Fellows or Cliff Brittle be elected to serve as Chairman of the RFU's Executive Committee.

Towards the end of a chaotic afternoon, after a seventy-minute delay for proxy votes to be counted, Brittle emerged the winner by 647 votes to 332, so defeating Jeavons-Fellows who was the RFU's preferred candidate and representative on the IRFB.

Quite apart from spectacularly misjudging the mood of those representing the game's grass roots, the question has to be raised: 'Why were the clubs asked to vote on this contest at all?' It is as if the shareholders at the Annual General Meeting of ICI, once introduced to the new Chief Executive, decided they did not like the look of him and voted instead for an unknown from a protest group out of sheer bloody-mindedness. Just as no company would allow the

Cliff Brittle (above) and John Jeavons-Fellows.

appointment of board members to be jeopardized in this way, the same should apply to any other major sporting organisation. Except the RFU that is.

Yet nothing unconstitutional took place at Birmingham on 14 January. On the contrary, in the RFU rules it clearly states under 13.1: 'There shall be six officers of the Union, namely a President and Senior Vice-President, a Junior Vice-President, the immediate Past President, an Honorary Treasurer and a Chairman of the Executive.' These it says, under 13.2 'shall be elected at each AGM or,' as clarified in 13.3, 'at a Special General Meeting'.

The first four appointees comes in the 'it's Buggins turn' category, and not much harm can be done by the elevation of this well-meaning quartet to irrelevant prominence, except that it perpetuates the legend of Bumbledom. But an Honorary Treasurer? Doesn't the multi-million pound RFU need a Financial Director in the age of paid players and mega-money television contracts? Should the committee not be able to appoint their own Chairman? Absurd as it may seem, apparently not.

Some members of the RFU's sixty-one-strong general committee must have wondered just what they had done to deserve such treatment. Others dismissed the Brittle affair as just a little local difficulty which would soon go away. If only.

Whether Brittle's seemingly effortless rise to power and authority will turn out to be the revenge of the small clubs and constituent bodies against the Executive Committee (all of whom voted for Jeavons-Fellows) remains to be seen. The episode bore many of the hallmarks of Margaret Thatcher's appointment of Dr George Carey as Archbishop of Canterbury to replace Robert Runcie. Those close to her, before one of her last acts as Prime Minister, said it was Margaret's way of exacting retribution from the General Synod, for all the opprobrium heaped on the Conservative government by left-wing Anglican bishops.

In the counties, however, there are those with long memories, who remember only too well what a hash the committee made over the sacking of England captain Will Carling the previous May. The humiliating climb-down handed far more power to the players and their agents than was ever envisaged or deemed wise.

What rankled most was the arrogance of the committee in expecting the RFU Commission's report – *Open rugby, the right to decide* – to be accepted without proper debate at the Birmingham SGM. Although the meeting agreed that the word amateur be deleted from the RFU's regulations, when it came to consider the Commission's report, delegates voted overwhelmingly to hold a second SGM to vote on whether English rugby should turn professional. For Jeavons-Fellows, the architect of the report, and the rest of the RFU committee, it was a thoroughly uncomfortable experience. It is doubtful if the Church of England could have made a bigger botch of things.

If the RFU expected a period of calm after the shambles of the two Birmingham meetings, they were soon very rudely awoken from their slumber. Following Sir John Hall's acquisition of Newcastle Gosforth, which gave the inflationary spiral its first twist, EPRUC proposed a club structure designed exclusively to make as much money as possible for England's top twenty-four clubs.

It is not relevant to pick over the arguments put forward by some clubs, or EPRUC. They have been rehearsed and amplified *ad nauseam*, taking acres of space in our newspapers. It suffices to say that if the RFU had produced a workable plan for the professional game, with a scale of payments within the limits of what clubs could afford – given perhaps some extra financial help from the RFU on the back of greater television revenues – we would not now be facing such uncertainty.

Instead we have a club game riven with greed, without restriction on the number of players not qualified to play for England, and a competitive structure which will do little for the development of the national side in the way the Super 12 tournament is doing so manifestly for South Africa, New Zealand and Australia.

When it seemed as if peace had eventually broken out between the RFU and EPRUC, it was only after a threatened breakaway had been avoided and the RFU acceded to the clubs' demands for a hefty chunk of all the new money pouring into the game. Were this to have been earned exclusively from participation in the televised Heineken Cup and the proposed Anglo-Welsh competition, no one would have minded. But, almost by the day, the RFU's troubles worsened.

The television companies who have played their part in destabilising so many sports – including rugby league – had no need to prepare an assault on the RFU themselves. They could safely leave that to the leading clubs, who set about the executive of the union with a ferocity which left the television managers open-mouthed.

The RFU President Bill Bishop stepped into an increasingly confused picture, looking just as Jim Callaghan did in the dying days of the Labour government in the 1979 winter of discontent, peering through his spectacles, groping to find a way out of the mess. Cast in the role of honest broker between the union and the clubs, the avuncular Cornishman never found the exit before his executive lobbed their most destructive bomb into the international arena.

With a year to run of the BBC television contract – worth £27.25 million, split equally four ways – the RFU signed a five-year agreement with BSkyB worth £87.5 million. The deal also included offers of £40.5 million to Wales and £28 million each to Scotland and Ireland. The announcement of the new arrangement provoked almost universal condemnation, especially from those justifiably concerned that Rupert Murdoch would now have control of the television rights to the two biggest annual competitions in world rugby, with the Five Nations being added to the Tri-Nations tournament.

Although Jeavons-Fellows was the RFU's representative on the Five Nations committee, the Celtic nations accused him of sitting in at home unions' meetings without saying anything about the RFU's decision to go it alone on a new television contract. Enraged by what they saw as underhand behaviour and dismayed at a perceived betrayal, the Five Nations committee decided to exclude England from the competition.

Since 1910 when Scotland joined the other three home countries in playing France regularly, the Five Nations Championship has been the proscenium arch of northern hemisphere rugby. In an act of wanton cupidity, England decided to

RFU President Bill Bishop with Secretary Tony Hallett. Perhaps the decisions made by the RFU hierarchy were not in the best interests of rugby?

pull out the largest cornerstone. The reaction of the other four countries was to organise a quadrangular competition played on a home-and-away basis, commencing in 1997. England were out in the cold, friendless and unwanted.

While struggling earlier in the year to contain the overweening self-interest of the clubs, the RFU held a strong moral hand, and could have counted on rather more support than they had imagined, before succumbing to the temptation of Mr Murdoch's gold. The RFU argued, not very convincingly, that they had every right to negotiate their own television rights. The extra money, the RFU contended, is needed to repay a £34 million loan advanced to fund the £66 million redevelopment of Twickenham. The clubs' share of the BSkyB payout is £22.5 million. This would provide each of the Division One clubs with £300,000 annually. Even then, EPRUC weren't satisfied; their members expected twice as much.

For the sake of the game's future, it must be hoped that a resolution can quickly be uncovered and the Five Nations saved. What we can be sure of is that the confusion, greed and unpleasantness is entirely of the RFU's making. Where it is possible to excuse Tony Hallett and Cliff Brittle of inexperience, their lack of sound judgement has been breathtaking. Why else would they have so naively endorsed the Bath-Wigan matches with such enthusiasm?

Does no one at Twickenham understand that rugby league is in such an appalling mess because it has, for the past thirty years at least, overpaid its players and underprovided for the paying public, who are now turning their back on the thirteen-man code in droves? For the most part the league game is played in slum conditions, with even the leading clubs struggling with mounting debt in decaying stadia.

There are valuable lessons to be learned from rugby league, especially for all those union clubs who are mortgaging their facilities to attract overseas players and finance overblown contracts. However, instead of warning their clubs of the dangers and highlighting the example of rugby league, the RFU welcomed the league's Chief Executive Maurice Lindsay to Twickenham like a visiting potentate, blissfully unaware of the widespread concern over Lindsay's leadership among those who still remain faithful to the northern game. In the process, the Rugby League, in general, were grateful for all the free publicity their game received and, Wigan in particular, for the generous contribution the receipts from the two matches made in reducing their £1 million-plus overdraft.

Before the IRFB's Paris Declaration on an open game, the RFU was in danger of fossilising a structure of inefficiency. The ineffective and outmoded concept of unpaid service is now totally inappropriate for an activity which has become a multi-million pound business within a growing sport.

In little more than a year since the professional era was trumpeted in, the principal officers of the RFU have hardly distinguished themselves by their competence, authority or acumen. Were they working in industry, the only other negotiations to be contemplated by this inept group would be over severance pay.

By the time this gets into print, heads may already have rolled. The next step will be bankruptcy for the clubs who have unwisely overreached themselves. All part of the price to be paid in pursuit of *auri sacra fames* – the accursed greed for money.

RUGBY WORLDWIDE

ALL BLACKS WIN THE FIRST TRI-NATIONS CUP

BY **BILL McLAREN**

Those are heady days for New Zealand. No sooner had Auckland gathered in the Super 12 trophy, following some scintillating action throughout the series, than the All Blacks took the inaugural Tri-Nations Cup by winning their first three games, to establish an unbeatable position even before they left for their final match in South Africa.

For the Tri-Nations Cup New Zealand, Australia and South Africa played a series of home and away games each Saturday between 6 July and 10 August. For long the southern hemisphere countries have envied their northern rivals' Five Nations Championship. Now they have set up their own competition, which also serves as a means of replenishing their coffers from which, among other things, they can pay their players. Points were awarded at four for a win, two for a draw, one for defeat by less than seven points and no points for defeat by more than seven points. There was also a special incentive to try-scoring by the award of a bonus point for four or more tries in a match.

It proved a highly successful format, producing perhaps the most devastating opening forty minutes of total rugby ever seen – by New Zealand against the Wallabies in the opening Test in Wellington – a tense, rivetting physical confrontation between the All Blacks and the Springboks in Christchurch and one of the most brilliant individualist tries ever witnessed, that by Australian full back Matthew Burke, against the All Blacks in Sydney.

The Test in Wellington was played in teeming rain, on a treacherous bog of a pitch and with a chill wind whipping from one end to the other. Yet, against the gale, the All Blacks, in a first half of almost perfect rugby, scored four superb tries and led by 25-6 at half-time against an Australian side of much talent and with David Campese, playing his ninety-sixth full international. Twenty minutes of fast, controlled handling action had passed before there was an All Black knock-on! They scored within eighty-five seconds of the start when, at a line-out, Robin Brooke, having switched places with Ian Jones in a pre-planned ploy, rose like a rocketting pheasant to exploit the new support law, whereupon a huge, black tidal wave swept over the Australian line for Michael Jones to get the try. There were others by the 'Paekakariki Express' Christian Cullen, the burly scrum half Justin Marshall, who used to work in a freezing plant, Zinzan Brooke, Jeff Wilson and Jonah Lomu, who appeared at various points to create as much damage as an earth remover. His ability to take out more than one Australian defender was a key element in fracturing opposition defence alignments. Andrew Mehrtens slotted three penalty goals and two conversions to beat Grant Fox's world record by reaching 200 points in just twelve internationals. Two penalty goals by Burke was the meagre reward for the Australians, shell-shocked at suffering their biggest ever defeat, 43–6.

A week later in Sydney, the Wallabies had the chance to atone against the

Springboks for that sad outcome – and they took it to end the South Africans' run of fifteen consecutive victories. The score, 21–16, owed something to the fact that the South Africans had had only one warm-up game against Fiji, whereas the Australians had played four internationals. Not only that, but the Wallabies had sought the assistance of the former rugby league internationalist Wayne Pearce to improve their tackling technique, and so well did he succeed that they made their tackling a formidable attack weapon. South Africa scrummaged well – they always do – but their finishing in their late rally was ineffective, especially against inspired Australian tackling in which Burke and the No. 8 Michael Brial set a splendid example.

Jonah Lomu charges through the defence of David Wilson in the opening game of the Tri-Nations series.

One highlight of another pulsating contest was the bullocking, forty-metres charge by the eighteen-stone Australian lock Garrick Morgan, direct from a restart kick, and the skilful dual role taken by their blind-side flanker, Daniel Manu, in fashioning a maul-over try by another young blood of high potential, Joe Roff. Joubert, not quite on song, landed a penalty goal before a tall farmer, fly half Henry Honiball, then took over the goal-kicking with two penalty goals and the conversion of a late try by Pieter Hendriks, after Japie Mulder had made in-roads and Joubert's miss-pass had given Hendriks a clear run-in.

So when the long-awaited New Zealand versus South Africa clash took place in Christchurch on 20 July, New Zealand already had five points, Australia four and South Africa just one. One of the most impressive features of the play of those two southern hemisphere giants is their defence organisation and their commitment to keeping the door closed. This, when allied to uncharacteristic New Zealand error and to both sides making far more use of the boot, made for far less continuity than in the two previous games. The South Africans were also penalised more often, mostly for creeping offside, so that Mehrtens proved the New Zealand match-winner with five penalty goals in their 15–11 margin, whilst Joel Stransky landed two penalty goals for South Africa who also scored the only try. It was beautifully conceived and created. Mulder made another of his bustling dents, Stransky, with rare vision, switched play to the right where Brendan Venter launched the man mountain Marc Andrews, who posed further threat before linking with Joubert, who scored. The South African full back had sprinted some forty metres from left to right in order to make the extra man.

The match had had a fiery opening when John Allan, the Glasgow-born South African hooker who previously gained nine Scottish caps, head-butted his rival Sean Fitzpatrick and should have been shown the door by Scottish referee Ray Megson, who received heavy criticism in the post-match assessments. Much of it was unfair. He did award some thirty-four offence kicks, twenty-two to New Zealand, and clearly displeased those in the southern hemisphere, who have become accustomed to their own referees opting out of certain laws in order to reduce stoppages and provide more continuous spells of action. There clearly is need for the International Board to consider, and soon, just how they want all of

Michael Brial was lucky to stay on the field after this altercation with Frank Bunce.

their referees to operate. Incidentally the unsporting behaviour of the New Zealand support at Christchurch was disgraceful, notably during South African goal attempts.

So the All Blacks knew that if they could beat Australia in Sydney on 27 July they would be the winners of the inaugural Tri-Nations tournament. They did just that with a thrilling rally from the dead that brought them victory in the last minute of a cracking contest that Australia were somewhat unfortunate to loose by 25–32. The Wallabies should have been reduced to fourteen players when Brial threw a hail of punches at Frank Bunce, the All Black centre, but was just cautioned by Scottish referee, Jim Fleming.

The Australians took the game to their rivals with unceremonious zeal, especially in the frontal areas, and led by 22–9 after fifty-seven minutes through tries by restored scrum half George Gregan and Burke, who also potted four penalty goals to three by Mehrtens. When Burke piloted over his fifth penalty goal for 25–15 with twelve minutes left it seemed that the writing was on the wall, but in the closing ten minutes the All Blacks found another gear in scoring seventeen points. In that quite breathtaking recovery, scrum half Marshall scored after Lomu had taken out five Australians and the match-winning try came from Bunce who crashed over after a move involving Mehrtens and Cullen. Mehrtens finished with twenty-two points from six penalty goals and two conversions to bring his tally to 248 points in fourteen Tests.

Undoubtedly the most thrilling bit of action in this splendid match was when Burke registered a solo try by using just about every form of deception. Stuart Barnes, the former Bath and England fly half, referred on television to the 'bravery and brilliance of Burke'. The bravery was when he exploded on to a situation of adversity as Tombs, in trouble, had to turn backwards in order to flip the ball into Burke's path. The brilliance was when he instinctively took off at amazing pace for such a heavy lad, veered out of the reach of Josh Kronfeld and Zinzan Brooke, outpaced Lomu and dummied Cullen before pinning his ears even further back to sprint home. It was a move that had been ignited some eighty yards away, although Burke said afterwards that his first reaction had been to boot the ball to touch and let his colleagues regroup.

The New Zealanders were now uncatchable with their thirteen championship points to five for Australia and just two for South Africa. But the Springboks still had opportunities to improve their final placing in their two home games.

New Zealand may be the southern hemisphere tri-nations champions, but the accolade for never throwing in the towel, no matter the dire adversity, must go to the Wallabies who plumbed the depths in their first game before hauling themselves back to a position of high respectability. On 3 August in Bloemfontein the Springboks seemed home and dry at 25-9 with just eleven minutes left. Yet once again the Wallabies, throwing caution to the wind, staged an absorbing revival that had even the renowned South African defence springing a leak or two.

They scored a gorgeous try through Ben Tune and lost by just 25-29 with the world champions glad to hear no-side blown.

The match was hardly the exhilarating spectacle of some previous games because the South Africans held to a restricted format, some fifty-one minutes having passed before they spun the ball from a set piece situation. The Australians were unable to break up the pattern imposed by their opponents until late on when they pieced together several bewildering passages of ball transference in which Pat Howard, operating at centre instead of, as usual, stand-off, proved clever and incisive with admirable support from those talented youngsters, Tune and Jo Roff. When Roff was left out of the original Australian side (he got into the game as replacement full back when Matthew Burke went off injured) there were critics who felt that the veteran, David Campese, should have been left out instead of Roff. Yet although Campese, in his 99th international, clearly showed that he is not as electric in his acceleration as he used to be, he made a number of classy contributions in keeping ball alive and in providing several good tackles notably one of copybook execution on the new South African speed merchant, Justin Smart.

When Burke departed, having put over a penalty goal from some fifty-five metres, John Eales, the Australian captain, again in splendid form, converted Tune's try as well as three penalty goals. The contest, however, proved a personal triumph for the Western Province stand-off, Joel Stransky, who took centre stage with all 25 points against Australia from six penalty goals and the conversion of his own try. That owed much to the sharp reactions of scrumhalf Johan Roux who committed his opposite number, George Gregan, before igniting Justin Swart on a sizzling touchline burst that ended with Campese's tackle. Swart, however, within the 'immediate' condition of the law, popped up the pass out of the tackle for Stransky, intuitively placed, to dive over. Stransky also asked hard questions

Japie Mulder is brought down short of the line by Tim Horan, with a little extra help from Daniel Manu.

of the Australian defence with a series of varied probing punts that set alarm bells ringing. There was also a rousing display by the Natal captain Gary Teichmann.

Just after halftime Johan Roux left the field after suffering an asthma attack and was replaced by that dangerous breaker, Joost van der Westhuizen. There had been suggestions amongst the ranks of the television pundits that all was not as it seemed, which in turn prompted the query: Is the era of the tactical replacement upon us as in football? Hopefully not!

New Zealand underlined their elite status as inaugural Tri-Nations champions in the closing match of the series on a soggy Newlands pitch in Cape Town when they gave South Africa a lead of 19-6 then took such control of virtually every phase as to fashion an astonishing 29-18 triumph in one of the most memorable internationals ever seen.

Sean Fitzpatrick with the Bledisloe Cup after New Zealand had beaten Australia in Sydney, a match that also secured the Tri-Nations Cup for the All Blacks.

In one particular spell of continuous action, the longest I ever can remember in forty-five years of broadcasting, there were some eleven phases, with the ball recycled then rippled through countless hands in the most bewildering fashion, as the All Blacks battered on the locked door of incredible South African defence before eventually it creaked open for two New Zealand tries of totally contrasting creation that, allied to the virtually unerring boot of the waif-like Andrew Mehrtens (five penalty goals and two conversions) brought about a New Zealand success that had appeared distinctly unlikely at halftime.

Just how influential to South Africa's downfall was the stretchering off of Francois Pienaar after fifty-four minutes was hard to say. In any event the South African effort

sagged as the All Blacks, in the words of their eighty times capped skipper, Sean Fitzpatrick, 'Just kept plugging away and it told in the last twenty minutes'. The New Zealand scrummage stood firm and their loose forwards, Michael Jones, Zinzan Brooke and Josh Kronfeld made far greater impact than their rivals.

Yet, earlier, South Africa had seemed focussed and clear about their conservative game plan built around their formidable pack, with its thirty-four kilos weight advantage, and the educated boot of Joel Stransky. They scored two splendid tries through Japie Mulder and Marc Andrews. Stransky potted two penalty goals and a conversion but missed the second conversion and another penalty that could have put the Springboks 20-3 up at halftime. However when Alama Ieremia replaced Walter Little after forty-three minutes, he effectively straightened every thrust and presented ball so well that New Zealand's loose forwards extended their control of later phases. They seemed permanently to have the ball and so developed continuity phases akin to seven-a-sides. Their mix of drive and spread spawned two cracking tries; one when Mehrtens looped Ieremia, Christian Cullen intruded like a meteorite and Glen Osborne came off his left foot three times to dot down a gem of a try, the other when Craig Dowd ended another lengthy siege by crashing over.

Thus the All Blacks won the Tri-Nations series that began and ended with the All Blacks on fire and coming near to perfection.

SPECTACULAR SUPER 12

BY **MILES HARRISON**

We all have them – friends who extol the virtues of their own favourite sport, but just cannot see the attraction of *our* number one choice. If you have ever been asked the question 'Why do you like rugby so much?' but have never quite been able to find the right words to do justice to the game's pace, power and skill, then I now possess the perfect answer.

The solution comes in three simple steps. First, obtain a video tape copy of the very best of the inaugural Super 12 series. Second, send the footage to the aforementioned doubting Thomas (recorded delivery is probably the best way as, when spreading the word, risks should be avoided). Third, and perhaps most satisfying, enclose a brief note along the lines of 'I told you so!'.

Rarely has a competition got off to such a rip-roaring start as was the case with the 1996 Super 12s. Admittedly, the concept was not revolutionary. The Australian, New Zealand and South African authorities built on the solid foundations established by the Super Tens. They could not have envisaged, however, the wave of interest which swept all the way from the Cape of Good Hope to the Tasman Sea. Almost one and a half million people attended over the three months of competition. This averaged out at more than 20,000 per game and five stadia dotted around the southern hemisphere, broke long-standing gate records for provincial or state matches.

The public liked what they saw as the sport was taken into a higher plane. Initially, many had been sceptical. The main questions were – would some regionalised sides receive the necessary support outside the insular environment of domestic rugby? – would the fear of failure to a team from another country produce stale and unambitious rugby? – and how would the players react to their new found status in the world of professionalism? The organisers need not have worried. Crowds flocked to see their local heroes play attacking rugby inspired by the bonus point system. Win or lose, if a team scored four tries in a match, they rightly got some reward. The coaches and players responsed well. They revelled in the opportunity to pit their wits against opposing national styles and the quality of the rugby produced surpassed all that domestic competition had previously offered. Perhaps most importantly, national selectors were given the chance to assess which players deserved the really big money as they watched them take part in what amounted to virtual Test match scenarios. On Friday 1 March 1996, a new age of world rugby officially began.

The opening day provided the first real hint as to the ultimate destiny of the trophy. The Auckland Blues showed great spirit to beat the Wellington Hurricanes, having to wait until three minutes from the end before taking the lead to win 36–28.

The adventurous tone had been set. The new laws, in operation for the first time in high-profile rugby, were proving to be a success. All forwards staying

down at the scrum and assistance to line-out jumpers creating quick off-the-top ball combined to create more room in midfield. The onus was once again on the attacking side to make use of the space provided. The laws were embraced positively, but the competition was not all sweetness and light.

The three countries involved have always had their own interpretation of certain aspects of the game. Nowhere is this better illustrated than with the tackle law. Consistency of refereeing is required, but not always provided. In addition, the use of neutral referees in international competition is now a must. Teams often left the field believing themselves to be hard done by, even if this had not been the case. Feelings of justice, however, were more profound when it came to the punishment of players judged to be guilty of foul play. A South African player was suspended for two matches after being accused of kicking the head of an opponent. Another South African got a seven-week ban for head butting. Yet an Australian had no further penalty after sending off was deemed sufficient following two ugly tackles which looked increasingly more distressing after every viewing. The point here is not that the tournament was littered with acts of violence, but that the responses lacked uniformity. It is an area for the governing bodies to work on.

These darker moments, however, were not the ones to linger longest in the memory. The Super 12 series was liberally sprinkled with sparkling matches and thrilling tries all far too numerous to mention here. But in the qualifying stages few will ever forget Natal's 63–25 hammering of Waikato. Also deserving of special mention is the Australian side the ACT Brumbies.

Auckland's Eroni Clarke smothers André Joubert as the Blues beat Natal in the final of the Super 12 at Eden Park, Auckland.

Dick Muir (Natal) and Craig Dowd (Auckland) struggle for possession in the Super 12 final.

They started unexpectedly well and only just failed to qualify despite a 70–26 victory over Otago on the final day of the league phase. Indeed ACT won one more match than fourth-placed Natal, but more tries won the day for the South Africans and they joined fellow countrymen Northern Transvaal, plus Queensland and the Auckland Blues in the semi-finals.

The top two teams gained home advantage, but for Queensland this proved to be of little comfort as a crowd of 23,000 saw Natal score seven tries. The hero in the 43–25 win was winger Cabous van der Westhuizen. His three tries capped a magnificent performance. A day later, the Auckland Blues played host to Northern Transvaal. Jonah Lomu started the second-half with another Incredible Hulk imitation. He carried three tacklers with him and scored a try to remember as the Blues won 48–11. The final had a Test match feel and Eden Park, with 45,000 cheering New Zealanders, was an inhospitable place for Natal. Auckland made an explosive start with Lomu once again in fine form. After twenty minutes, the Blues led 20–3 but much to Natal's credit they pulled it back to 20–16 at half-time. This only served to spur Auckland on to greater things and by the end of the match they were coasting with young flanker Andrew Blowers scoring two of their six tries. Auckland ran out 45–21 winners.

There were many stars of the tournament and all three countries can look forward to a bright future if the likes of Christian Cullen (Wellington), Wayne Fyvie (Natal) and Elton Flatley (Queensland) continue to progress.

It seems a little unfair that some sides had the advantage of six home fixtures in the qualifying stage. Inevitably, time zones played their part and jet lag, coupled with a tight playing schedule, hit certain teams. But those who saw and marvelled at the first year of Super 12 rugby have been left hungry for more.

WHAT FUTURE FOR THE HONG KONG SEVENS?

BY **IAN ROBERTSON**

For the twenty-first year in succession Hong Kong once again became the global centre of world rugby as twenty-four countries sent their top rugby players to take part in the Cathay Pacific Hongkong Bank Sevens.

The tournament has come a very long way since the early days when it was held in front of a few thousand people in the old football club stadium. Now 40,000 join battle to snap up tickets for the Sevens every year in the palatial surroundings of the magnificent new Government Stadium.

They have been rewarded with some truly superb rugby, produced by the world's greatest players, in the most exciting venue imaginable. In 1996, the standard was as outstanding as ever and the Government Stadium – a small green oasis in the middle of a huge concrete jungle – reverberated to the exuberant cheering of the capacity crowd as hundreds of tries were scored in thrilling fashion over two and a half days of competition. A total of 2,638 points were scored and there was a whole series of excellent matches in the Bowl and Plate competitions, as well as in the more rarified stratosphere of the Cup.

Arguably, the loudest cheers were heard in the early stages of the tournament when a handful of the minnows managed to score a try against one of the really big fish. Both Canada and USA scored tries against the current fifteen-a-side world champions South Africa, and there were also tries for Korea against Australia, Malaysia against Ireland and Sri Lanka against France. Such memorable moments have always been the pure magic of this great rugby extravaganza and it is this huge cross-fertilisation of so many different rugby cultures that makes the Hong Kong Sevens so breathtakingly unique.

It is impossible to state too strongly the importance of the opportunity afforded to the smaller emerging nations to rub shoulders one week every year with the giants of world rugby. It is an unforgettable experience for the lesser-known players to meet and mix with the greatest names in rugby, on and off the pitch, for the best part of a week in the biggest and best sevens tournament in the world.

There are so many ingredients which make the Cathay Pacific Hongkong Bank Sevens so special. The exotic venue is stunning. The two sponsors have supported the tournament with a zeal that very few major sporting events around the world can match. The PR company Prism headed by Des McGahan and Marlene Lee, has always been aware of the needs and the power of the media.

All twenty-four teams stay in the same hotel and have done since the inception of the competition. In the days leading up to the pool matches, they all train and practise together. That makes for a very friendly atmosphere which is perhaps the most significant single element in explaining why every top player in every country enjoys these sevens so much.

My real fear is for the future. 1997 is safe because that is when the World Sevens is in Hong Kong. But it is hard to see the 1998 tournament in Hong Kong attracting anything like the quality of players of recent years. The new professional game amongst the major International Board countries will make it well-nigh impossible for the top players to gather in Hong Kong as they have done in the past. The southern hemisphere Super 12 series has already resulted in Australia and South Africa sending drastically under-strength sides. The same will almost certainly apply in the future to England, Scotland, Ireland and Wales.

There is a breathing space of a year before decisions have to be taken, but with the Five Nations Championship destined to finish in April in 1998, there is little doubt that the Hong Kong Sevens cannot survive at the end of March. Fortunately the Hong Kong Rugby Union is well aware of the problem and they can canvass a lot of opinion before deciding what to do.

For a diehard traditionalist like myself, one hopes the great bastions of the past like British Lions tours and the Hong Kong Sevens can be saved for ever, but the omens are not that good.

Another world star is born. In 1994 it was Jonah Lomu, 1996 saw the arrival of Christian Cullen on to the world rugby scene.

Suffice to say that some of my best memories in recent years have come from the Sevens and I'm delighted to report that 1996 was no exception. So often a new name explodes on to the scene and captures all the headlines. It happened with a couple of unknowns called David Campese and Mark Ella in the early Eighties. In 1994, the world caught a first sighting of Jonah Lomu at the Hong Kong Sevens. In 1996 it was another New Zealander who stole the show – Christian Cullen.

He proved to be the complete all-round sevens player with a potent mixture of blistering acceleration, sustained searing pace and the ability to side-step and swerve past even the most determined defenders. In full flow he was a glorious sight to behold and everyone in the Government Stadium knew instantly that a new rugby star had arrived.

Once again, Chris
Sheasby showed the
Hong Kong crowd
what a complete
player he is.

By comparison the rest of the New Zealand side were merely outstanding and so it was no surprise that they successfully defended the Cup they had won in 1994 and 1995. If Cullen was extra-terrestrial in his exploits, Jonah Lomu, Eric Rush, Glen Osborne and Peter Woods were all magnificent. It is worth travelling 6,000 miles to see a sevens side of such thoroughbred quality.

In the pool matches in just fourteen minutes they rattled up seventy-five points against Sri Lanka, seventy-seven against Japan and twenty-eight against France. Add to that forty-nine against Ireland in the quarter-finals and forty-two against England in the semi-finals and it is easy to understand how they were described all weekend as irresistible and unstoppable.

To be fair, Fiji ran them very close in the final only losing 19–17, but there is no doubt that the New Zealanders are currently the best sevens side in the world.

Fiji scored 157 points in their three pool matches and then had wins over Wales and Australia to reach the final. Winners in Hong Kong seven times, Fiji remain a major force at sevens rugby.

Among the teams which disappointed were the Australians, the Western Samoans, the South Africans and the Scots. Scotland invented the game of sevens, but that counted for nothing as they lost to England and Argentina in the pool matches. That put them into the Plate where they made a hasty exit in the quarter-finals to the French. France followed up with wins over South Africa and Hong Kong to win the Plate.

For the third year in a row Ireland played some great sevens rugby to reach the later stages of the Cup competition, but there they ran into the full might of New Zealand and that rather abruptly ended their challenge. Wales also performed with great credit to reach the Cup quarter-finals before losing 28–12 to Fiji, and they had the satisfaction of producing two of the best players in the whole tournament in scrum half Rob Howley and wing Ieuan Evans.

Perhaps not surprisingly England turned out to be the best of the northern

THE HEART OF ASIA

We serve the most dynamic part of the world with over 650 fligh

CATHAY PACIFIC

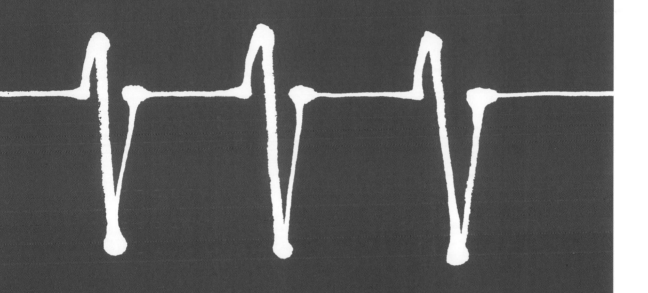

week to and from Hong Kong. Cathay Pacific. The Heart of Asia.

hemisphere teams. They were the best-equipped for sevens rugby and they are, after all, the defending World Sevens champions. Chris Sheasby showed again just what an excellent sevens player he is, and a complete footballer. It amazes and disappoints me every year that he is never seriously considered for the full England fifteen-a-side team. He is better at the line-out than any of the current England loose forwards, quicker in the open, solid in defence, and he is a tremendous support player. Hopefully one day his chance will come. The New Zealanders felt that he was good enough to be an All Black being similar in build and speed to Michael Jones and Josh Kronfeld and that ought to mean something to the England selectors.

Among the backs Damian Hopley and Austin Healey caught the eye on many occasions, and under the watchful eye of the England manager Andrew Harriman, the man who captained the winning England World Cup seven in 1993, and coach Les Cusworth, the English can be very satisfied with their efforts. They can also look forward with a fair degree of optimism to defending their world trophy in Hong Kong in 1997.

That should be one of the great sporting events of the year. It is only fitting that the Hong Kong Rugby Union should host such an exciting and prestigious tournament because they have nurtured the game of sevens with immense care and pride for the last twenty-one years. This is their reward and it is richly deserved. Each year the Hong Kong Sevens has gone from strength to strength. 1997 promises to be the best ever.

Captain Eric Rush and Player of the Tournament Christian Cullen celebrate New Zealand's third win in a row in Hong Kong.

LEARNING THE HARD WAY – Scotland in New Zealand

BY BILL McLAREN

Rob Wainwright and his Scotland tour party did not exactly set heather on fire during their eight-game expedition to New Zealand in May and June, and returned home having had to accept once more the brutal fact that a gulf still exists in the pace and style of Test rugby between the northern and southern hemispheres.

In losing the two Tests – 62–31 in Dunedin and 36–12 in Auckland – the Scots were unable once again to record a victory over the All Blacks, their record now stands at eighteen defeats and two drawn in twenty meetings.

True, the Scots won accolades for the manner in which they sought to take the game to their renowned opponents and achieved the notable feat of scoring more points in a Test against the All Blacks than any other country – thirty-one in Dunedin on 15 June. All the same, in losing both Tests, the Scots scored five tries but conceded fourteen. Of course, the Scots already had seen on their television screens some of the Super 12 matches and had marvelled at the pace and continuity achieved by the competing sides, not least by their exploitation of the new scrummage and line-out laws and a form of lenient refereeing that made for fewer stoppages and lengthier passages of action than ever achieved in the Five Nations.

To their credit, the Scots did seek to emulate the more entertaining style of play they had adopted in the 1996 Five Nations Championship, and were encouraged to do so by their coaching duo, Richie Dixon and David Johnston, under the paternal gaze of Scotland's Rugby Director Jim Telfer. Naturally it took the Scots some time to adapt to the changed laws with which their opponents were quite familiar. Nor did Scotland possess quite the cutting edge available to New Zealand through their sensational new full back Christian Cullen who, in the space of a fortnight, scored ten tries in three Test matches, through Jonah Lomu, predictable but still a mighty force, and through Jeff Wilson, a quality footballer who had scored three tries and a conversion on his début at Murrayfield in 1993.

Gregor Townsend took some of his thrilling Five Nations form into the first Test, including a marvellous loop-try, before having less success in the monsoon conditions at Eden Park in the second Test. There was, too, the comeback of Gary Armstrong after missing nineteen internationals, and he still showed all the tenacity, grit and acumen of old, regardless of opposition or conditions. But whilst the Scottish forwards covered themselves in glory, especially in the first Test when they actually had the better of the ruck-maul statistics, the threequarters could not match the the incisiveness that marked the New Zealand back's ability to provide space – especially for Cullen who gave a telling

Kenny Logan finds space during the second Test, played in monsoon conditions at Eden Park, Auckland. New Zealand ran out 36–12 to take the series 2–0.

demonstration of his gifts of deception and strength on the run. Townsend did manage to ask questions in conjunction with his loose forwards, of whom Wainwright gave an impressive lead, but the All Blacks had the stronger strike force. Not only that, but there was further evidence of how New Zealanders make their tackling an offensive weapon with 'big hits' which either catapulted the ball-carrier backwards or dislodged the ball. As one example, Rowen Shepherd, who had a successful tour, not least as a goal-kicker, achieved forward momentum before being swept backwards some fifteen metres in a tidal wave of black jerseys.

In the first Test it was the creation of space and the ability of the All Blacks to come on to the pass at pace that proved the big difference between the two sides. In the second Test, the All Blacks made the scrummage a key weapon. In atrocious conditions and on a waterlogged pitch, the vaunted Auckland front row of Craig Dowd, Sean Fitzpatrick and Olo Brown (with 129 caps between them), frequently undershoved their rivals, sometimes in a fashion now outlawed on grounds of safety. It proved a testing time for the new Scottish cap, Barrie Stewart of Edinburgh Academicals, on the tigh-head side. That astute New Zealand coach John Hart, had not only appreciated the value of a strong scrummage under the new law, with its insistence on all eight forwards staying bound until the scrummage is over, but also that Scotland were playing a young prop, just twenty-one, and short of genuine international experience. Apart from the unrelenting pressure from a New Zealand scrummage that contained six Auckland forwards, Hart had created a repertoire of scrummage ploys that were both impressive and effective. Four of their five tries in Auckland were launched from scrummages and all were scored by loose forwards, a luxury Scotland could not match as their edifice squeaked and swivelled in trying to stay on terms with powerful opponents.

Apart from driving home to the younger Scots that there are no easy games in New Zealand, even against second or third division opposition, the tour also underlined that there is a vast difference in the approach to refereeing between the two hemispheres. It was clear that the southern hemisphere referees were not greatly concerned about how the ball was won at line-outs, rucks and mauls, just so long as it was delivered. Line-outs were contested in jungle warfare conditions with a case of every man for himself. Nor were officials fussy about players going to ground and working the ball from there or about players blocking off in front of their ball-carrier. It brought home to the Scots that it was even more important to play, not to the laws, but to the manner in which each referee interpreted them. It had to be some advantage that New Zealand sides were well acquainted with the style adopted by their own officials.

It also was significant that concern has been expressed down under by, among others, the New Zealand coach John Hart, that northern hemisphere referees had been appointed to take charge of some of the Tri-Nations games. The fear is that officials from the four home unions will be too strict and so will create a stop-start style that will not be acceptable to audiences recently fed on a diet of all-action, entertaining rugby.

The New Zealand tour saw a welcome return to Scottish colours for former Lions scrum half Gary Armstrong.

Delight for French captain Philippe Saint-André as France beat the All Blacks in the first Test.

touring team – a massive 43–9 victory at St Johnstone's football ground.

Thereafter, their tour rather fell away and disasters were more frequent, ending with a 55–0 loss to England 'A' followed by a better, but vain, challenge to a full England side who were at their least enterprising, at Twickenham (27–9).

Meanwhile, the All Blacks had visited Italy and France and returned home with seven wins from eight games, the only defeat coming in a Test match against France, with the hosts running out 22–15 winners. They paid them back a week later in Paris with a resounding 37–12 victory and also beat Italy in an earlier Test 70–6, so the steamroller was only briefly halted.

Another visiting team before Christmas was Transvaal who played five matches, winning two and drawing one, while in the early New Year New South Wales completed eight games all over the British Isles and won all but two of them – the losses being against England 'A' (24–22) and Ulster (40–33).

Before that England's Colts had conquered all in Canada (six played and six won) but the strength of the Canucks was amply demonstrated by their national Colts team who held the excellent English to a 15–12 margin of success.

New Zealand and Australia both hosted off-season tours in 1996 with Scotland offering stout but unavailing opposition to the All Blacks in losing two Tests gallantly (Bill McLaren reports more fully on Scotland's tour elsewhere in this book). They won four of the eight games overall, but Wales could only manage three victories aginst relatively weak opposition in a similar number of matches in Australia, where apart from two heavy Test defeats they also lost to New South Wales, Australian Capital Territory (a real emerging force) and Australia 'B'.

Canada also failed where Wales had been dismembered, winning only two of their five matches against modest opposition and being thoroughly trounced in the only Test against the Wallabies (a massive 74–9 scoreline).

France were the only European country to thrive on tour, although they had to

recover from the initial shock of defeat at the hands of a Buenos Aires XV (29–26). After that setback they avoided further disasters and were convincing winners of the two Tests in Buenos Aires (34–27 and 34–15).

It is an irony that the home countries are still on a learning mission where the art of modern rugby is concerned. Jim Telfer, Scotland's guru, openly expressed his belief that an improvement can only come if all countries would virtually organise summer season tickets to the southern hemisphere from now onwards.

Above *Steve Williams breaks away from the scrum during Wales's defeat in the first Test in Brisbane.*
Left *Sam Payne and Dan Crowley move in to win possession as Gareth Thomas goes to ground in the Sydney Test.*

CELLNET.
THE ELITE SPONSOR OF THE
ENGLAND RUGBY TEAM.

Call 0800 21 4000 for details of what Cellnet can do for you.

THE NET THAT SETS YOU FREE.

A NEW STYLE
OF RUGBY

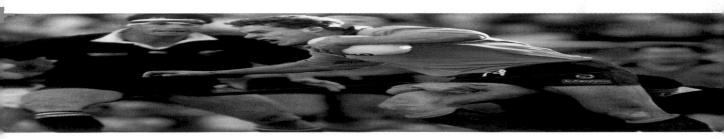

THE COACHING IMPLICATIONS OF THE NEW LAWS

BY IAN McGEECHAN

Having watched games from the southern hemisphere, the new law changes have undoubtedly been instrumental in producing a more fluid game. They challenge players, coaches and referees to be positive and make things happen.

Interpreted correctly, everything is geared to moving the ball quickly from breakdown situations and freeing up ball for supporting players. Three changes in particular are significant

1. All eight forwards to remain in the scrum. This will get rid of the midfield clutter of breaking back rows once the ball has been lost. It puts the onus on scrum halves and No.8s to release ball quickly and attack spaces either side of the scrum. Defending back rows and midfields will have to close this space quickly, assuming that the No. 8 or scrum half has already successfully crossed the gain line. The threat of attacking this space means that it is more difficult for the backs to drift early across the field and, subsequently, leaves space on the outside for the wings and full backs.

It is interesting to note that the southern hemisphere sides are already trying to turn defensive scrums away from the easier breaking side of left to right. Powerful front rows and genuine scrummaging is definitely back in play.

Similarly, the role of the defensive scrum half has been shackled by way of restricting him to defence within one metre of the scrum unless he retires behind the hindmost foot of his own pack. Scrum halves, like Joost van der Westhuizen, can no longer move across into midfield.

Around the scrum a number of players are now required to make decisions to produce a concerted defensive blanket; a half-second delay by any one of four players will hand the initiative to the attackers.

2. The second major change is in the duty of the tackler after he has gone to ground – he must immediately release and roll away from the tackled player and the ball. This should keep a space around the ball for supporting players to come in and play the ball on their feet, rather than falling on top of the two players lying on the ground.

For a long time this had been a messy part of the English game and, for me, the referees tended to protect players on the ground rather than penalise them. Here is a great opportunity to keep supporting players up. One interesting thought: should the referee allow more licence to the attacker to free up the ball whilst being strict with any defender who is not on his feet? Is this 'spirit' rather than law?

It is this law change more than any which could instigate the more fluid play which everybody now demands.

3. The third change is the ability to 'lift' in the line-out. Supporting players can now grasp the jumping player to keep him in the air. Somehow I do not think

Ian McGeechan takes charge during the Lions tour to New Zealand in 1993. Will the home nations adapt to the new laws in time for the trip to South Africa in 1997.

British referees will allow the freedom which is now common practice in the southern hemisphere. Having said that, it was interesting to see the New Zealand props holding the jumper's shorts by the leg to hoist him as the ball arrived while Ed Morrison was refereeing. It would seem that northern hemisphere teams can only hold above the waistband – we shall see. My concern is that the southern hemisphere teams may develop new jumping and lifting techniques which will be very difficult to combat in the next World Cup. Is that a level playing field? It will certainly encourage the development of lighter second rows!

There are a number of other changes which are not as significant, but nevertheless enhance the view that movement in the game is to be encouraged.

Scrum halves are now allowed to put one foot past the ball at scrums to help them get a quick pass away – but they are not allowed to dummy pass at all from rucks and mauls, or from scrums.

Only the back player can leave the scrum, and only then if he is picking up the ball. It will be interesting to see how the referees interpret 'binding' for the defensive back row. As the southern hemisphere season has progressed, arms have got longer and grips looser.

Finally, on tap penalties or free kicks the cavalry charge is not permitted within ten metres of the try line – the old American football scenes have gone! However a team can retire beyond the ten metres and still set up the charge.

On quickly-taken tap penalties, retiring players cannot interfere with the opposition, but can get involved once a player who was ten metres back comes forward.

All in all the challenge is there for players to be sharp and positive in keeping the game fluid; and for referees to respond in spirit to the players who are trying to play, whilst being strict on those who try to slow the game down by being in the wrong place at the wrong time.

I just hope referees have the confidence to use the laws as guidelines and give everybody the positive platform on which the game's progress relies.

FACING THE FUTURE WITH NOKIA.

Nokia Telecommunications is at the forefront of tomorrow's technology, developing the solutions to meet the needs of the next generation.

Nokia believes in encouraging achievement, and has built its business on respecting and caring for people, whether customers or suppliers, staff or friends. In our own way we each help to build a better future for everyone, and as part of this Nokia is happy to support the work of The Wooden Spoon.

NOKIA
CONNECTING PEOPLE

Nokia Telecommunications Ltd, Lancaster House, Lancaster Way, Ermine Business Park, Huntingdon, Cambs PE18 6XU, U.K.
Telephone +1480 434444 Fax +1480 435111

THE NEW COACHES DOWN UNDER

BY **ALASTAIR HIGNELL**

JOHN HART (New Zealand)

John Hart confronts the media, as he settles in to the job he always wanted.

All it needs is a bow-tied master of ceremonies inviting the audience to be amazed and advising young children not to attempt any of the routines unless under strict supervision.

A New Zealand training session is much more a public spectacle than a painful technical run through, much more showtime than grunt and groan time. The All Blacks go through an increasingly complicated and injury threatening series of practices at breathtaking speed with ferocious concentration. They move swiftly from one practice to another, rarely stopping for a drinks break, never stopping to question an instruction. Fitness conditioner Martin Toomey puts them through their paces, selectors Gordon Hunter and Ross Cooper patrol the perimeter like a couple of stern-faced senior prefects, and John Hart plays ringmaster, cracking the whip and cracking the jokes with perfect timing.

The public love it, especially when Hart keeps changing his mind about which tackle bag he wants prop Olo Brown to hit. They gasp with him when flanker Michael Jones almost cuts one bag, and the man holding it, in two, and they roar encouragement with him as new full back sensation Christian Cullen shows astonishing athleticism in knocking down one target after another after another.

It's pure theatre. It's also pure John Hart. The fifty-year-old Aucklander has waited a long time to become the All Blacks coach and he is determined to enjoy every minute of it. Sober-sided New Zealanders thought that the style that took Auckland to unprecedented success in the mid-eighties was too loud and too flamboyant for the All Blacks. His partnership with grim-faced Grizz Wyllie during the 1991 World Cup was an uneasy alliance. When Hart lost out to Laurie Mains immediately after that tournament it seemed that the articulate Aucklander was destined to remain a prophet without honour in his own country.

But Hart, who was passed over on four separate occasions, obviously thought the post of All Black coach was worth waiting for. The New Zealand public will be glad he did. As rugby enters the new professional era, with new laws and new opportunities, Hart is quite obviously tailor-made for the job.

John Hart discovered a new world-beater in Christian Cullen – for the Kiwi coach, rugby remains a young man's game.

Like all New Zealanders he is obsessed with winning. For Hart though, style is almost as important: 'I was fortunate to coach a great Auckland side in the mid-eighties, a fifteen-man side using the ball and kicking very little. I've always had that attitude to the game. My personal view is that the All Blacks lost their way for a number of years and forgot about using the ball. They found it again in some parts of the World Cup and I think we've got to get back to that because I think it's a game we play well and it's a game the New Zealand public enjoy.'

Hart is not that far removed from his predecessors to the extent that he believes

in style above everything else. Winning is still the highest priority but entertainment comes a pretty close second: 'In this modern era of professional rugby, you have to think about entertainment but, to me, it's not much entertainment if you are losing. I have always believed in winning, but I always hope any team I coach will win in style. I never set points targets. After we ran in sixty-two against Scotland in the first Test this summer, people kept asking me what we were aiming for next time. I said I didn't care if we scored only twenty points as long as we played very well and as long as we played to our potential.'

And, provided Hart can unearth some tight five forwards in the next couple of years, the potential of this All Black side is huge. Hart, of course, did inherit an exciting, exhilarating team that failed only at the final World Cup hurdle. It was Hart's predecessor Laurie Mains who launched Jonah Lomu on an unsuspecting rugby public, and introduced bright young stars like Andrew Mehrtens and Josh Kronfeld. But in full back Christian Cullen, Hart has unearthed another gem and he is committed to the belief that more than ever rugby is a young man's game: 'It has always been a philosophy of mine. At one stage with that great Auckland side, I think eighty per cent of the team had been brought in at twenty-one years or younger. But it's not just a question of finding them. You have to understand them and introduce them in the right way, and not take risks with them. I was very confident that what we had done with Christian Cullen was sufficient to know that he would be able to handle it. But I also set a base for him so that if it didn't work out for him at the trial, that if he didn't make the All Blacks, it wouldn't mean that he had failed. I think it's all about how you handle them. I think they respond well to that.'

Hart's determination to give youth its head extends to helping his young stars come to terms with life as the first full-time professionals: 'The demands on the All Blacks have always been huge. But the new professional era has made new demands and I believe it is our duty to help the players cope. We have to help them with their management of time, the management of their life, the nurturing of opportunities beyond rugby, and not praying on the altar of rugby football. To do so a player can come to grief pretty quickly at the whim of a selector or injury, so we have to to make sure the players understand that there is life beyond rugby, and that they have got to continue to grow as people and not just as rugby players. Some have had difficulty with that, but only a few. I'm really impressed with the attitude of the All Blacks at the moment, in terms of meeting their media requirements, their sponsorship requirements and especially their training requirements. That's what we've got to keep the focus on.'

Hart especially believes his players' responsibilities also include presenting a smiling, friendly face to the public. They are not all as erudite as their coach, but they are, without exception, approachable, affable and apparently willing to submit to seemingly endless inquisition by the media. It wasn't always so.

'I was with the side in the UK for the World Cup in 1991 and it really hurt me when I saw the attitude of the media to the All Blacks and I could understand why. As a team you just can't act like that, not in the professional era. You have to be media-friendly, media-inclusive and I've set in place a whole programme to accomplish that. Yet there have to be boundaries, and I think keeping to those is as much a challenge for the media as for the players. I keep telling them your fans are important and the only way to get to your fans is through the media.'

In fact Hart is positive about just about everything to do with his job. He realises that the thinking behind the new laws fits perfectly his vision of the game: 'I think the new laws, especially regarding the scrum, have created a different mentality. Inadequate sides could survive in the past by packing the defence but now it's much harder and every player has to be a split-second decision-maker, able to react to any eventuality. The line-out laws have also been a revelation. Basically they have ensured that the backs get more ball and that they have the space to use it. As we have seen in the Super 12 series, they've been great for rugby.'

In the short space of time he has been in charge, Hart has been great for the All Blacks. Manager, motivator, communicator he has been just what they have needed off the field. He is determined to leave his mark on it as well:

'Professional rugby is going to be enduring and therefore, in New Zealand, we have got to ensure we do it well, from the beginning. We have to play consistently well and that is based on consistency of selection. That hasn't happened in the past. There have been too many changes to the All Blacks and that has affected the security of the players. I've promised them that we are going to pick consistently. In return we demand consistency from them. That's difficult because we have such a punishing schedule. With ten Tests in thirteen weeks we're having to develop as a team and as players in the full glare of internationals. That's hard especially as we are all conscious of just how important the All Blacks are to be people of New Zealand.'

The people of New Zealand need not be too concerned. At the dawn of the professional rugby era, the All Blacks are in the best possible hands, the hands of a man dedicated to winning with style and humour, prepared if necesssary to face defeat with dignity. Cometh the hour, cometh John Hart.

GREG SMITH (Australia)

When Australia visit Scotland and Ireland this autumn, they bring a new coach, a team in transition and a tried and tested approach.

Forty-six-year-old former English teacher Greg Smith is the man in charge. He has a hard act to follow. His predecessor as coach to the Wallabies was Bob Dwyer, the longest-serving coach in international rugby. Under his guidance Australia won the World Cup at Twickenham in 1991 and dominated international rugby until South Africa and England beat them in the 1995 tournament.

That was a series too far, both for Dwyer and many of his players. Most of the team edged out by England had either retired, been injured or lost form dramatically by the time of Smith's début as Wallaby coach, the first Test against Wales in June. No Phil Kearnes, Rod McCall, Tim Gavin or Willie Ofahengaue in the forwards, no Michael Lynagh, Jason Little or Damien Smith in the backs, only Tim Horan and the ageless and indestructible David Campese to give some sort of continuity. Fifty-six points in the first Test and another forty-one in the second suggested that new coach and rookie internationals had clicked instantly.

'My philosophy, put simply, is to play the game at pace. I want my players to do anything they can to up the tempo of the game. I think that's crucial in beating teams. I liken modern rugby to arm-wrestling. If you can really increase the pressure in terms of the amount of time the ball is in play, then fatigue is going to become a factor. Unless people are training for that sort of fatigue, there are going to be patches in the game where they really struggle. You do that by keeping the ball in hand, playing to your support players, keeping the pressure on the opposition, keeping them moving, keeping them guessing.'

Smith knows the sort of players he needs to play the sort of game he demands. The forwards have to be mobile, the backs have to be penetrative: 'It's important

Australia's new coach, Greg Smith (left) shares a drink with Prime Minister John Howard after the Tri-Nations clash with South Africa at Sydney.

to me that they can all break the line. We pick a team and from numbers nine to fifteen they must all be blokes who can do some individual damage, rather than the old stereotype of a rugby team where the five-eighth (fly half) has a good catch-pass game and can kick for territory. We want a number ten to be a running five-eighth too. A player like Rob Andrew wouldn't be much good to me. I'm not degrading what he's achieved, because he has achieved remarkable things in rugby, I'm just saying that in the kind of rugby we want to play, he just wouldn't fit in. He would dislocate the team.'

The selection of a team to match Smith's version has already begun. Exciting young backs have been drafted in, Smith controversially opting to experiment with Joe Roff at centre against Wales instead of the more predictable Danie Herbert, Sam Payne has been tried out at scrum half, the highly rated Ben Tune on the wing. In the forwards, mobile front-rowers Marco Caputo and Richard Harry have been blooded and Owen Finnegan given a run on the flank. These are selections with World Cup 1999 in mind, although Smith points out that he himself has only got a two-year contract. He refuses to be patronising towards northern hemisphere nations, but he does see this autumn's tour as a further chance to try out new players and new ideas. The heavier grounds will not only provide a taster of World Cup 1999, but will also provide a challenge to Smith's high speed style of play.

'We've found that playing night Tests, when there's dew on the ground, has made it difficult to play the way we want to. But we are determined to cope. We may have to make adjustments for the heavier grounds in Europe. We'll be trying hard to maintain pressure on the opposition through retention of the ball, but we won't do it regardless. We're not silly people.'

For all that he's new to role of international coach, Smith is still too cagey to be drawn on whether his playing philosophy will also be challenged by European referees. According to public opinion down under, those officials are perceived as a cross between Torquemada and the Marquis de Sade. While his New Zealand counterpart John Hart decried the decision to allow northern hemisphere referees to take charge of this summer's Tri-Nations series on the grounds that they lacked sufficient familiarity with the new laws, Smith restricts himself to observing: 'There's no escaping the fact that sport is a big entertainment business and rugby is a product we can market throughout the world. Referees are a crucial part of the whole thing. Like the players, and the coaches, they should be evaluated very strictly. One of the most important things is their fitness, their ability to stay with the pace of the game. It's a very difficult game to referee if you are a fit person. If you are not, it becomes a nightmare.'

According to Smith referees are not alone in being exposed by the new laws and by the approach to them: 'The back-row law has forced defences to be more disciplined. They have to be mentally, conceptually able to cope with whatever

Greg Smith believes that his world-class players such as Jason Little and John Eales (inset) need to be protected from the ever-increasing demands of international rugby.

circumstances throw up. In that sense, it changes the back row you'd pick. The slow No. 8s have had their day. If you have to carry somebody who's light on pace, he'll have to play on the blind side. Numbers seven and eight have got to be pacy players. In that sense, and in the sense that the new line-out laws make it advisable to keep the ball out of touch and in play, the game has radically changed.'

The Super 12 series has proved that beyond doubt. Down under they talk of little else. The competition grabbed the public's imagination and the breathtaking rugby it produced fired their souls. Smith, though, is not a wholehearted convert: 'Sure, there was some pretty good rugby played, but there were also some pretty bad games. The problem from my point of view was that Australia had three teams, playing three different kinds of rugby.'

However the pluses far outweighed the minuses. Traditionally Australian selectors have only been able to pick from two teams. If you didn't come from New South Wales or Queensland you had little chance of wearing the gold and green. The inclusion of the ACT Brumbies in Super 12 competition has enabled many more players to demand attention. Indeed Smith's first international team contained more Brumbies than New South Wales Waratahs or Queensland Maroons. If Roff was the most high-profile of those, new caps Marco Caputo the hooker, back-row man Owen Finnegan and converted fly half Pat Howard can be even more grateful to Super 12 for their selection.

'The series has been a marvellous guide. The selectors this season have been given a better view of players than ever. Some of the matches have been as difficult, if not more difficult than Test matches But there are dangers. I am concerned about the demands we are making on our top players. You can't just ask a player to run one thousand times up a mountain and assume he will keep on running. He won't. He will eventually break down. I want to see our top players getting the right amount of rest – maybe they should be barred from playing for their clubs for a month either side of internationals. The task is for us to protect the world-class players we have got, and I would put lock John Eales and centres Jason Little and Tim Horan in that category, and at the same time develop a squad of twenty-five to thirty players capable of playing for the Wallabies in any Test at any time.'

There is no doubt that Smith's Australian team will be as welcome to these shores as their predecessors. But even though in his scheme of things, the Tri-Nations, the Bledisloe Cup and the World Cup are all-important, Smith won't be taking Scotland and Ireland lightly.

'There is no chance of that. It's always dangerous to treat an international match as an experiment. Having said that, we are in the process of rebuilding. We have to make changes as we go along because when you are rebuilding, you don't always get it right right away. Form fluctuates, especially for young players, and you have to read those fluctuations. Nevertheless I hope to have a settled side by the time we reach Scotland and Ireland this autumn.'

And the team he brings will be as exciting and entertaining as Australian teams of the past. Smith can promise that: 'I think we should have a fairly defined style of play by then, and the sort of team playing the sort of rugby people will enjoy. I want the players to enjoy it, and I want the crowd to enjoy it. It's the only way to go.'

ALL BLACK MASTERCLASS FOR JIM TELFER

BY **ALASTAIR HIGNELL**

Jim Telfer – Scotland's Director of Rugby – believes that northern hemisphere countries have much to learn from New Zealand's approach to the game.

Jim Telfer is no George Peppard, but a Scotland win against New Zealand must now seem even more like Mission Impossible. It's ninety-one years since the two sides first met and for the last thirty of those Telfer has made it a personal crusade to down the All Blacks. Statistically at least, he is further away than ever. New Zealand posted a record score against Scotland in this summer's first Test and even though a rainstorm ruined the second Test in Auckland, the All Blacks still ran in a further five tries. Scotland it would seem are further off the pace than ever. Telfer would not agree. There are indeed lies, damned lies and statistics. Scotland scored five tries of their own in the two Tests, they dominated play in both games for long periods and, according to New Zealand skipper Sean Fitzpatrick, at times they had the All Blacks rattled.

Telfer needs neither kind words nor excuses. Since that first trip thirty years ago he has been an admirer of New Zealand rugby. Since that first trip he has modelled his rugby philosophy on the All Black's and he has learned all that he can from them.

The message he comes back with is always the same: 'I would advise the rest of the world to get down here. To go on tour to the most fanatical rugby nation on earth, take on the local teams and learn. It's tough, it's not always enjoyable, but it's something you've just got to experience.'

It was even more important for Telfer this time round. New laws and a new competition had revolutionised the southern hemisphere's autumn. Crowds at Super 12 matches had been ecstatic. Telfer had to see for himself.

'The new laws have produced a game that is very enjoyable to watch. They've put the emphasis on quick thinking by all the players. They've challenged all coaches, and, in particular, all referees, to approach the game in a very positive manner. I can see some disadvantages, particularly relating to the third man in the tackle. Referees in New Zealand tend to let everything flow. I don't think there will be so much leeway back home. While in one sense it's good that the laws at the set-pieces have been devised so that a team is almost certain of winning its own ball, I'm worried that some of the contact situations are now hardly contestable. Teams stay in possession longer so you have to have very good organisation in your defence and make sure you don't panic. We didn't do that in the second Test, where we defended well, but we were a bit naive in the first Test. Certainly when you do have possession, you have to make it count. We didn't do that, the All Blacks did.'

In particular Telfer refers to the law requiring flankers to stay bound at the set scrum. The All Blacks scored twice from that position in the first Test, while three of their five second Test tries came from scrums. Because of the conditions in Auckland, those scores all came from close range, but according to Telfer the new law has equal implications for the men out wide: 'We've said all along that the back three would become a far more potent force than they were. What has also surprised us is that the scrum half and No. 8 now have much greater roles to play.'

To take advantage of the new regulations players have to be fitter, harder, better prepared and, a theme Telfer has returned to constantly in the last three decades, more like New Zealanders: 'In New Zealand, if you don't win physically, you don't win at all. We've learned you have to be very strong in the tackle, in contact situations, in ball retention. The level of skill of some of the players in the provincial games has been higher. Our players have to build themselves up, play in competitions that demand they work harder on their bodies. In international rugby we assume that players are strong and fit and skilful but, in the end, it is the mental approach that wins the day. Scotland has to be harder, more streetwise. We are not ruthless enough. In the second Test we scored two tries, but didn't look like scoring any more. That is where the All Blacks are superior to us. They get to within five metres of the line, and that's where they stay until they score.'

Away from the Tests, Scotland had big wins against moderate opposition in Blenheim and Wanganui, scraped to victory in Rotorua and Invercargill and lost narrowly to the more powerful, but by no means most powerful, unions. Despite that Telfer was reasonably satisfied with Scotland's progress: 'Most of our players have come on during this tour. I think we have adapted pretty well to the new laws. It might have been more difficult if they didn't suit the sort of game we have been trying to play. It has always been our goal to develop continuity, recycle possession and keep the ball in play. I think that at times we showed the All Blacks that we have got what it takes to play international rugby. In the second Test I think we had them under pressure for a time. They looked human and I thought that at only 17–7 down and with the gale at our backs, we could have won. But you have to applaud the All Blacks. They hit back immediately and took their chances.'

The tour was also about Scotsmen taking their chances. Scotland picked several young players to go to New Zealand, primarily for the experience. Telfer reckons they've all benefitted enormously: 'The three young forwards (lock Scott Murray and props Tom Smith and Barrie Stewart, who was capped in the second Test) have impressed me with their commitment. In the backs, Ronnie Eriksson made his debut in the first Test and played most games on tour. He and full back Stuart Lang have learned more than anyone.'

Telfer is confident that all his players now know what it takes to succeed in international rugby. He is happy to let the physical conditioning experts raise their fitness to the required levels. He is convinced that there is only one way to raise playing standards. In the club/district debate, he insists that the clubs are non-starters. He admits that this too is a recurring theme: 'I have been saying it for the last thirty years. Provincial rugby is the only answer. If we are to go forward we have to have fifty or sixty players competing regularly at the same level, be it in the European Cup or whatever. If necessary, we will use a draft system to ensure that all the players we want to look at are exposed at that level.

That includes those playing for clubs in another country, as long as their contracts allow.'

That idea may be too radical for some, and it may buck the northern hemisphere trend towards club rather than district combinations, but in New Zealand it is already happening. Jonah Lomu wouldn't have played in the Super 12 series if the New Zealand Rugby Union hadn't alligned Lomu's National Championship side Counties with Auckland. By the same token the Waikato Chiefs were able to call on Frank Bunce from North Harbour while Christian Cullen was drafted from Manawatu to play for the Wellington Hurricanes. While that is beginning to sound like the divisional championship that is so maligned in England, the second tier district sides in New Zealand have also succumbed to merger mania. Hawkes Bay, proud conquerors of the Lions only three years ago, have signed a letter of intent with Manawatu and all but voted themselves out of existence. Both unions are prepared to take the hard decisions in order to stay afloat financially and to prevent their young talent being creamed off by wealthier rivals.

That is the sort of ruthlessness that Telfer can only applaud. It is the sort of ruthlessness that if applied consistently in the northern hemisphere might just produce a team to match the All Blacks. Telfer knows that and he desperately wants that team to be Scotland. He wants a team that won't self-destruct inside eighty minutes. One suspects he will keep going back to New Zealand until he finds out how to produce one.

Derek Stark is stopped in his tracks during Scotland's match against Wanganui. According to Jim Telfer the tour to New Zealand was a necessary part of the learning curve.

RUGBY'S
TWO CODES

GORY, BLOOD-SOAKED COMBAT BETWEEN MONSTERS, FREAKS AND HIDEOUSLY DEFORMED BEASTS.

(NO IT'S NOT SATURDAY AFTERNOON AT THE STOOP.)

Tackle the very latest in hi-tech attractions in The Adrenalin Zone at the Trocadero. Segaworld, Virtual World, Virtual Glider, Showscan's Emaginator, Funland and Lazer Bowl. And after you've finished rucking and mauling with them you can always try Madame Tussaud's Rock Circus, Thunder Drive or Planet Hollywood. So you can see how a visit to the Trocadero kicks all other days out into touch.

THE ADRENALIN ZONE

No.1 PICCADILLY CIRCUS, LONDON. TELEPHONE: 0171 439 1791.

THE ORIGINAL RIFT

BY DAVID FROST

The date of 1895 is well known as the time when twenty or so leading rugby union clubs in the north of England, mostly in Yorkshire, broke away from the Rugby Football Union and formed the Northern Football Union, subsequently – since 1922 – the Rugby League. It was indeed on 29 August 1895 that these clubs met at the Mitre Hotel, Leeds and decided to secede from the RFU. But the rumpus over 'broken time payments' – compensation to players who missed work through playing rugby – had been going on for several years before that.

The RFU, determined to keep the game strictly amateur, had had to hold many time-consuming enquiries into allegations of broken-time payments to the players in the North where it seemed natural to many people that compensation should be paid.

A crucial date was 20 September 1893 when, at the RFU General Meeting at the Westminster Palace Hotel in London, two members of the RFU and Yorkshire committees, JA Miller and M Newsome, proposed and

Above *William Cail, President of the RFU in 1893.*
Left *David and Evan James, brothers and Welsh international half-backs, who were professionalised by the RFU in 1893 after they had been 'persuaded' to move from Swansea to Manchester club Broughton Rangers.*

G. Rowland Hill, Secretary of the RFU in 1893, and (below) the Rev Frank Marshall.

seconded respectively 'that players be allowed compensation for *bona fide* loss of time'.

The RFU anticipated such a move and, thanks largely to one HE Steed of Lennox FC, gathered votes and proxies for an amendment 'that this meeting, believing that the above principle is contrary to the true interest of the game and its spirit, declines to sanction the same'.

Some contemporary writers believed that this meeting in 1893 was the real moment of the split because, although the northerners are said to have come down to London in two special trains, the RFU's amendment was carried by 282 votes to 136.

Following that meeting in 1893, the RFU, bolstered by their vote of confidence, drafted a host of strict laws banning professionalism. These were due to be voted on at the General Meeting of the RFU on 19 September 1895. Three weeks before this meeting the leading clubs in the North held their meeting in Leeds and resigned from the RFU. Subsequently the RFU's 'laws as to professionalism' were passed, and the Northern Football Union took root and flourished.

It is not easy, in 1996, to appreciate fully the effect of the split more than a hundred years ago. But the facts speak for themselves. The England team of 1892 won the Triple Crown without having a single point scored against them. That team was made up of eight players from Yorkshire, three from Lancashire, two from Durham, one from the Midlands, one from Somerset and none from the London area. England did not win the Triple Crown again for twenty-one years. In nine seasons after 1896 England's record was won six, drawn three, lost eighteen.

Yorkshire, who won the County Championship – taken very seriously in those days – in five consecutive years from 1892–96, did not win it again until 1926. Their northern rivals, Lancashire, champions in 1891, did not win it again until 1935.

Because of the split the number of Yorkshire clubs in membership of the RFU fell from 150 to fourteen. In 1893 the RFU had 481 clubs; in 1896 there were 383; and in 1903 there were 244.

The advent of professionalism in 1995 and 1996 would surely make the Rev Frank Marshall – staunch upholder of the principle of amateurism in Yorkshire and England and the author of the definitive 500-page book on the early days of rugby union, published in 1892 – turn several times in his grave. Was he right?

THE UNTHINKABLE COULD HAPPEN

BY **BRIAN ASHTON**

Bath versus Wigan at Twickenham was not the first time the two rugby codes had met under union rules. Two matches took place during World War Two, one at Headingley, Leeds, the other at Odsal Stadium, Bradford. The league players won both games. Several commissioned officers played in the union teams – the league teams were composed entirely from men in the ranks. A social commentary on the two games at the time perhaps! There were, of course, special wartime circumstances surrounding these matches and it was ridiculous to think that anything remotely similar could ever take place again as life returned to normal after 1945.

Anno Domini 1996, therefore, was a momentous year for the two worlds of rugby league and union. Bath played Wigan twice under both league and union rules/laws. Wigan also played in and, predictably, won comfortably the annual Middlesex Sevens tournament at Twickenham. 1996 saw the advent of a rugby league Super League and the implementation at senior club and international level of professionalism in union. Is there a pathway being cleared for the two codes to reunite after just over one hundred mostly hostile years apart?

I think that the answer is yes. When this may occur is much more difficult to forecast, but I believe that sooner rather than later two or three Super or Premier Leagues playing the game of rugby under one set of laws. Bath, Leicester, Harlequins, Wigan, St. Helens, Bradford Bulls in one league – a mouthwatering prospect for true rugby fans everywhere.

What mental abberations, some of you may be thinking, have led me to this conclusion?

Bath's Brian Ashton and Wigan coach Graeme West in conversation before the historic match at Twickenham.

John Sleightholme displays the power and speed that had made him one of Bath's most effective players in the first match, played under rugby league rules.

1. The sharp-edged social images of the cloth-capped league brigade and the stiff-shirted union old buffers have all but disappeared, except in the eyes of a few diehard administrators and supporters of both camps. These images, incidentally, have rarely been as readily apparent to the players.

2. The economic structure on the playing side of both games is now very similar. An élite group of players at the top of each game are being paid to play. The vast majority in each game remain amateur. The money division therefore has disappeared.

3. Rugby union, as a spectator sport, needs revitalising as it enters the professional world. As I write it appears that the changes in the laws to improve the playing image (a trick surely borrowed from rugby league) have had a beneficial effect in the southern hemisphere Super 12 tournament. Will this translate to northern hemisphere rugby union? The answer will be revealed in 1996–97.

4. A unified game combining the best elements of both codes would provide a much better spectacle on the field and far more enjoyment for players and paying spectators.

5. A game that retained the essential elements of each code would be an historic, new and exciting challenge to the players. Top players, in any sport, respond to top challenges and in rugby the challenge could not be bigger than being successful in the new unified game of rugby.

6. Both league and union are now competing in the professional world. Will the commercial market be able, or wish, to support two separate games of rugby? There is no precedent for this in any other sport – no two separately-managed professional variations of soccer, cricket, tennis etc. It may turn out to be commercial nonsense for the two codes of rugby to remain in competition.

Below are some of the rules/laws I believe would be crucial in developing a new game.

A. No line-outs
(i) If the ball is kicked over the touchline on the full then the non-offending side will receive a free kick at the point from which the original kick was made.
(ii) If the ball bounces in play before crossing the touch-line then a scrum takes place at that point with the non-kicking side getting the put-in.
(i) and (ii) apply anywhere on the field of play and should sharpen up the kicking game and make it far more positive.

B. Number of players
The great British compromise (a trait readily associated with Northerners) means that teams would have fourteen players – seven backs, seven forwards.

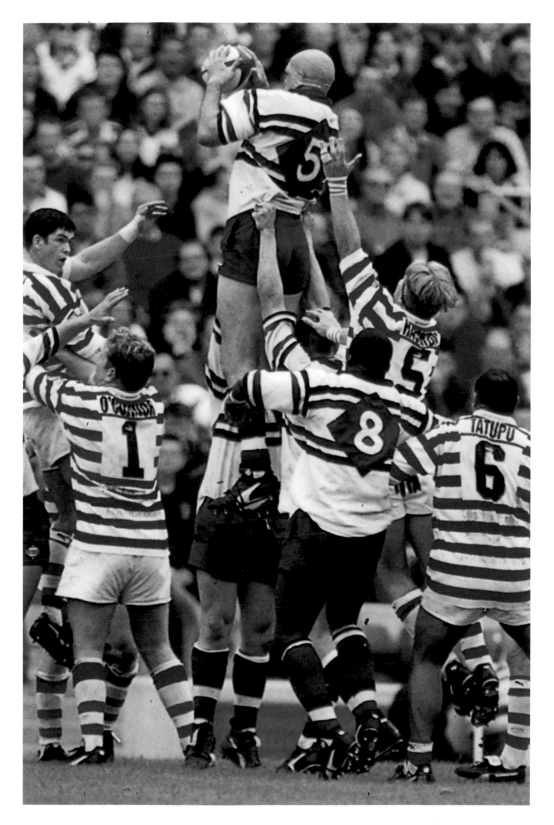

Bath show Wigan how to win ball in the line-out, but these skills could become obsolete if the two codes were to combine.

C. Scrummage

The scrummage will take place under the present rugby union laws. There will be, of course, only seven players packing down. The two back row players *must* scrummage in the rugby union channels of blind-side and No. 8. This means no open-side flanker to practise disruptive and negative tactics.

D. The tackle

The six tackle rule to apply as in rugby league.

(i) If a player is tackled but remains on his feet the game continues until:
 (a) he goes to ground
 (b) the referee shouts 'held'.

Other players may continue to drive him forward as in the rugby union dynamic maul. If the ball is moved away from the area before the referee calls 'held' then no tackle is recorded. The 'held' call will occur when the maul comes to a stand-still.

This should encourage the idea of keeping the ball alive and in play.

(ii) When the player is tackled to ground then a play-the-ball takes place as in rugby league rules.

E. Discipline

The sinbin and associated disciplinary rules of rugby league apply.

After the violence of the 1970s the League game has done a remarkable job in cleaning up its image.

What was once unthinkable has already happened – a rugby league side at Twickenham.

F. Points-scoring system

Try	5 points
Conversion	2 points
Penalty	3 points
Dropped goal	1 point

CONDITIONING FOR A COLLISION SPORT

BY JOHN KEAR

John Kear, Coaching and Academy Executive at the Rugby Football League.

With the recent 'clash of the codes' when Wigan RLFC met Bath RUFC at both rugby league and then rugby union, sandwiched around the successful appearance of Wigan at the Middlesex Sevens in May 1996, much debate and controversy has ensued about the relative merits of both codes of rugby. Obviously there are insular traditionalists on both sides of the fence who feel that neither code has anything to learn from the other. However, most fair-minded and far-sighted sports people can see that there is much to be gained from an exchange of ideas in the preparation of élite teams for maximum performance in whatever sport.

Since the appointment, in 1982, of Phil Larder as Director of Coaching, British rugby league has always adopted an open-minded approach with the sole aim of improving playing standards domestically whilst seeking parity with the top rugby league-playing nation, Australia. Much research has been carried out looking at the southern hemisphere, investigating other sports, especially American football, and also in the early nineties the Rugby Football League commissioned a study by Andrew Clarke, then a student at Liverpool. This study asked élite players for information relating to various aspects of the game and one of the main conclusions was that the players felt that the overriding cause of fatigue appared to be related to the collision, i.e., being tackled when in possession of the ball, or carrying out a tackle when not in possession.

At this point it is worth noting that in a game of rugby league, the ball is actually in play for over fifty minutes and there are over 300 collisions within that period. It is obvious that physical contact with other players is very demanding for all involved. Many coaches now believe that winning the battle of the collision in both attack and defence is a vital ingredient of success for any rugby league team, and this is reflected in emphasis on techniques and conditioning in training programmes.

Returning to the aforementioned study, the players involved in the questionnaire were of the opinion that fatigue reduces a player's power, i.e., his ability to be strong and fast. Tired players are unable to accelerate

Always ahead of the pack...

as quickly and collide with the same intensity, and fatigue would obviously lead to a general deterioration in performance in the battle of the collisions. Although subjective opinions, these views must be taken into consideration as they were the opinions of the best players in the country at that time.

A video analysis project was then implemented to study the physcial requirement for playing rugby league and this centred on the critical element of play – the collision. Players were individually filmed during British first division games as well as in a Test between Australia and Great Britain at Sydney in 1992. Using a slow-motion video (fifty frames/second) the researcher was able to note accurately the players' activity.

Warrington's Mark Jones feels the effects of a collision with Andy Farrell and his Wigan team mate.

The aspects of offence that were analysed were:

1. The mode of forward locomotion that the ball-carrier was in when he took possession of the ball (i.e., walking, jogging, striding or sprinting), and the duration of the movement in 100ths of a second;

2. The mode of forward locomotion that the ball-carrier was in when he collided with the defenders (i.e., walking, jogging, striding, sprinting), and the duration of that movement in 100ths of a second;

3. The part of the ball-carrier's body where the defenders collide with him (i.e., front upper, rear upper, front lower, rear lower);

4. The number of defenders involved in the tackle;

5. The distance moved in the collision, in metres. This was either plus (towards the defender's goal line), or minus (towards the ball-carrier's own goal line) and

represented the distance that the ball moved from the first contact with the first defender to the position where the ball was subsequently played;

6. The duration of the collision in 100ths of a second. This was divided into two parts; the first part was an analysis of how long the player could remain on his feet in the collision, and was recorded from the first contact with the first defender to the point when the ball-carrier's upper body hit the ground; the second part was analysis of how quickly the ball-carrier could restart play, from the movement his upper body made contact with the ground to the point when he subsequently played the ball with his foot;

7. The result of the offensive collision: was the attacker held on his feet or grounded?

The aspects of defence that were analysed were:

1. The mode of locomotion that the defender was in when he collided with the ball-carrier (i.e., standing, walking, jogging, striding or sprinting), and the duration of that movement in 100ths of a second.

2. The distance moved in the collision, in metres, from first contact to last contact.

3. The duration of the collision in 100ths of a second, from first contact to last contact.

4. The result of the defensive collision: was the defender standing or grounded, and on top of or below the ball-carrier?

A summary of the findings showed that successful teams:
- ran onto passess more quickly than their opponents
- approached the collision more quickly than their opponents
- remained on their feet in the collision longer than their opponents
- made more ground towards their opponents goal line in the collision
- regained their feet after the tackle more quickly than their opponents
- required more defenders to halt their progress than their opponents
- approached the defensive collision with greater speed than their opponents
- lost less ground as defenders in the collision than their opponents.

Physical prowess plays a major part in determining results and it is seen as essential that players in successful sides have excellent upper- and lower-body strength, outstanding power in the collision and endurance to withstand the effects of the collision.

Strength, speed, power, endurance and flexibility are prerequisites to being a top rugby league player. These apsects of a player, along with the commitment, technique and size allow the result of the collision battle to be determined.

Weight is largely genetically determined, although it can be altered through correct diet and training habits. Speed and strength are both components of

power. Speed can be trained in the appropriate way, while raw strength can be successfully developed in the gym, and then, with the correct strategies, used to increase power. Endurance of the muscular, aerobic and anaerobic types is also essential, so that the collision in the eightieth minute is as intense as in the first.

Wigan celebrate their success at the Middlesex Sevens.

Commitment is up to the player himself and his hunger for the battle – in many cases this is part of his character – while technique can be mastered through good coaching.

In conclusion, to cope with the intense physical demands of a collision sport, a programme of conditioning is a necessity which, allied to other aspects of team preparation, will allow athletes to display their tremendous power, acceleration and stamina, characteristics so evident in Wigan's performances against Bath and at the Middlesex Sevens. To fully investigate such a programme in a text of this length is impossible, however, rest assured all élite rugby league teams address *Conditioning for the Collision* as an essential part of preparation for the game of rugby league.

John Kear is joint author of Conditioning for Rugby League *and author of* Skills Development for Rugby League – *both titles to be published by Queen Anne Press in October 1996.*

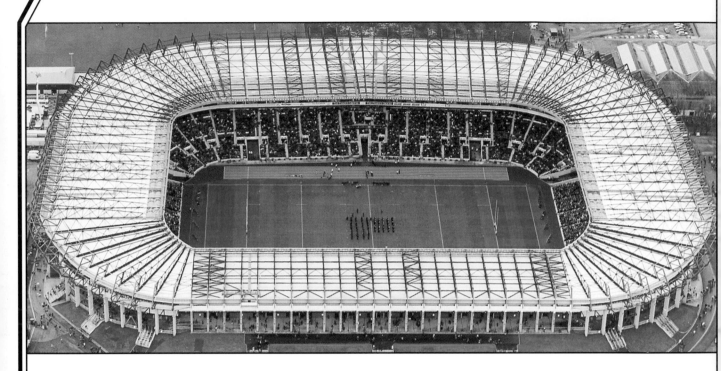

ON THE
HOME FRONT

WILL CARLING

BY **MICK CLEARY**

Was he born or was he made? Did England make Will Carling great or did Will Carling make England great? These are the only questions to ponder now that the most famous cleft chin in the rugby world has headed down the tunnel for the last time. Or at least he has as captain – the most successful ever in the game with forty-four victories from his fifty-nine games in charge. He still intends playing on, as fly half of all things. He'll probably draw a headline or two in that role. It's a sure bet too that his name won't be out of the gossip columns for long either. His alleged affair with the Princess of Wales will see to that. He may have denied everything, his marriage may have broken up, but the paparazzi don't give up that easily. Their commitment is for life.

In many ways this little titbit, sad and tawdry as it may be, captures so much of Will Carling's worth and significance. Not the fact that he could land a princess, if he ever did, but that anyone anywhere should think an England rugby

The start of an era. Will Carling offloads the ball during his first match as captain versus Australia in November 1988.

captain worthy of mass media attention. Bill Beaumont is far more famous for his role in BBC's *Question of Sport* than he ever was for his role in an England shirt. You don't think so. Then name any of the captains who came between Beaumont and Carling. Got past Nigel Melville and Richard Hill yet? What about John Orwin? Or John Scott? Or even Richard Harding? Now, they are all, in their way, worthy rugby men, but none of them raised more than a flicker of interest outside a clubhoue bar. Carling was different.

It was not that he stood out from the crowd in any particular way when Geoff Cooke made that now famous phone call in November 1988. Carling, who had won his first cap earlier than year against France, thought Cooke was going to tell him he'd been dropped. Instead Cooke was telling him that, at the age of twenty-two, he was to be the youngest England captain for fifty-seven years. England beat Australia ten days later and the roller-coaster adventure was underway.

Why Carling? Not even the man himself knows. He's vowed that he will one day sit Geoff Cooke down, pour a good few drinks for themselves and then get him to answer that one question: why me? Cooke himself might not come up with much of an anwer. His original intention when he had come into office twelve months earlier had been to base his side around the captaincy of Nigel Melville. Then Melville was injured. Who next? You have to consider just what Cooke was seeking from the team to appreciate just what he was seeking from his captain. Cooke wanted stability, order, consistency, self-belief and drive. Carling was young, gifted, ambitious and personable. It was, of course, an inspired choice born out of judgement, but also of luck. What might have happened if England had lost to Australia? What might have happened if Carling had been forced to give in earlier to the shin splints which eventually forced him to miss the British Lions tour to Australia the following summer? Neither came to pass however. As they say in the military, the one ingredient a general must have is luck. Cooke must be credited with seeing what Carling could offer.

The fact that Will Carling could gain the respect of the likes of Brian Moore, Wade Dooley and Paul Ackford said a lot about his captaincy skills.

Any yet Carling was never to be the most astute tactician in the heat of battle. Too many games went begging – Cardiff 1989, Murrayfield 1990, World Cup Final 1991 – for Carling ever to be acclaimed as a great strategist. He himself is right to see the shaping of a game as a collective activity. But when the heat really

Carling rounds the last line of defence to score against Wales at Twickenham in 1990.

*The good times.
Time to celebrate
England's third
Grand Slam in five
years.
Disappointment was
to follow in the
World Cup later in
the year as they
crashed out to New
Zealand in the semi-
final.*

comes on, when the pre-match parameters become blurred in a flurry of fierce action, it is then that a real captain defines himself. Buck Shelford managed it, so too did Nick Farr-Jones. Sean Fitzpatrick has had great success of late as both a motivator and as one able to gently tilt the tiller in another direction.

No, Will Carling did not have this level of perception. This is a fine level of criticism. Of course, Carling gave direction and shape to so many of the matches in which he played, and in which England played with thrust and style. That they scored a record number of points in the Five Nations Championship (118 in 1991–92) under his leadership is often overlooked. Nor could England have won three Grand Slams in eight years without a little bit of shrewd input from Carling. What he lacked was the extra edge, the almost indiscernible something which separates the great from the very good. Willie John McBride, Shelford, Farr-Jones were great captains: Will Carling was a good, an extremely good one.

There was no great mystique about what he did. Sure, there were gimmicky little innovations such as handing out press-cuttings prior to the Calcutta Cup match of 1991 just to remind the boys how painful it really had been the year before. He often sent personalised notes to players on the eve of matches, pointing out just what their contribution meant to the side. But many people might have hit upon these little stunts. Not all the receipients would have believed in them. For some reason with Carling they worked. The very fact that some hard-edged old campaigners – Peter Winterbottom, Wade Dooley, Dean Richards among them – stuck by Carling through all the turblulent times, never bad-mouthed him in private or public, suggests that Carling had a vital commodity – credibility. There was something of the public school caricature about him. From prep school to Sedbergh to the Army; father and brother both military men; job later in the City; club, Harlequins – it was a tailor-made C.V., one which would alienate as many people as it might impress. Carling was far more than a cardboard cut-out however. He had guts, ability and a necessary aloofness. If only because of Cooke's endorsement, Carling represented stability. The rest of the team were more than happy to go along for the ride.

There were bad times, notably in the early nineties when he thought of giving up the captaincy. On the Lions tour in 1993 his form dipped. He was dropped for the first time in his career and he thought of coming home, but he stuck with it. He came through the 'old farts' affair in May 1995 with, if anything, his reputation enhanced among the rugby public. He battled through his personal difficulties at the start of the 1995 season and played some of the best club rugby of his life. If nothing else these peaks and troughs illustrated just how hard Carling worked to secure, sustain and improve his captaincy. Few things come naturally to anyone. It is only those prepared to mix the perspiration with the inspiration who make the grade. As for the other conundrum, as to whether he made England or vice-versa, the final words, as ever, might be best left to Brian Moore who once said of Will Carling: 'He gets too much credit when things go right and too much blame when things go wrong.'

Now, it's someone else's turn.

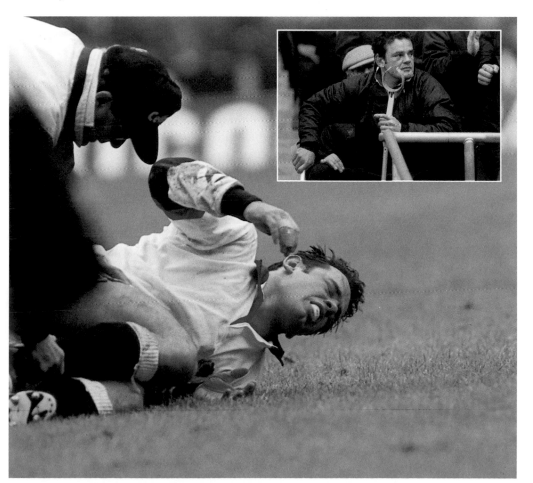

The final moments for Carling as captain were spent writhing in agony with a twisted ankle that forced him to sit out the remainder of the match against Ireland in the stands.

MORE ENTRIES FOR THE HEINEKEN CUP

BY **BILL MITCHELL**

One of the innovative features of the 1995–96 season was the inaugural Heineken Cup for Europe, which was played over a three-month period during November, December and January, ending with a final at Cardiff Arms Park, in which Toulouse – the tournament's best team – narrowly defeated Cardiff after a high-quality thriller.

Initially, a dozen teams took part – three clubs each from Wales and France, two from Italy and one from Romania plus the Irish provincial representatives of Leinster, Ulster and Munster. England and Scotland were not represented, but the excitement involved has encouraged both to enter sides in 1996–97, although like Ireland, Scotland will be represented by three Inter District sides – South of Scotland, Edinburgh and North & Midlands – in the revised four pool format (five teams in each pool).

Scotland's most successful Inter District team was, in fact, the Exiles, but their players might have been required by their club sides, which would have made their appearance an impractical proposition. The Irish presence remains unchanged with the same three sides, of whom Leinster, semi-finalists in the last campaign, were the most successful.

France have made changes for the next tournament, but still include Toulouse, the holders and favourites to retain the Cup, along with Brive, Dax and Pau, all of whom enter on the strength of their national championship performances, while Wales retain runners-up Cardiff, their cup winners Pontypridd, Heineken League champions Neath and Llanelli. Italy once again has two entries in Milan and Benetton Treviso.

With no representative from Romania this just leaves England, whose first entrants have been selected on Courage League positions – or is it on the basis of Pilkington Cup performances, since the two finalists also topped the league tables? No matter as both Bath and Leicester are in along with Harlequins and Wasps.

The European competition organisers took another leaf out of the soccer book by introducing their equivalent of the UEFA Cup, called the Conference. This allows some deserving cases to be included in international club competition with France and Wales having seven places each, England six and Ireland (Connacht), Romania (Dinamo Bucjarest), Scotland (Glasgow District) and Italy (Petrarca Padova) one each. In this there will be four pools once again, but each will have six sides and both will require five sessions to complete the preliminaries before the knock-out stages.

The final winners are hard to predict, but one suspects that, in both competitions, neither the Scots, the Irish or the Italians will be strong enough.

In the Conference the French hand looks to be the most powerful with such famous names as Agen, Toulon, Castres and Bègles involved. Wales's best chance

would seem to come from Swansea, while one would look to Northampton to provide England's strongest challenge.

The Heineken Cup is, however, an altogether more open affair and, while Toulouse remains the team to beat, one can expect strong challenges to come from Cardiff (again), Bath, Leicester and Pontypridd who, having broken their 'duck' in terms of domestic competitive success, can only get better, particularly if they can retain their best players. Neath have lost many of their side from last season and must rebuild, so they will be lucky to make a major impression.

Celebration time for Toulouse as they become the first winners of the Heineken Cup. How will the likes of Bath and Leicester fare in the 1997 competition?

Whatever one may feel about the new professional game, one must say that competitions which bring together Europe's top clubs can only be a good thing and we would hope that television's response will be for the good and not merely a way for clubs to grow rich without giving anything in return. Clubs have a big responsibility to the game even though the fact that they will mostly be on satellite television will restrict the number of viewers.

It is an exciting prospect if last season's pioneer competition is a reliable guide.

GOOD IDEA, WRONG TIME – The Sanyo Cup

BY **ALASTAIR HIGNELL**

Right idea, right place, wrong time. That was the received wisdom when it was first mooted that the Courage League champions should play an exhibition match against a World XV at the end of April at Twickenham.

It was obvious that Leicester would be involved in the run-in to the league title. Few doubted that, provided they avoided Bath in the earlier rounds, they would also be odds on to appear in the Pilkington Cup final. Everybody suspected that the World XV would, faced with the competing demands of Super 12 and a French international against Romania, struggle for players, and that those players, given only a handful of training sessions, would struggle for cohesion and identity. Most of us were wrong.

An estimated 35,000 festive supporters not only exceeded the expectations of the match organisers, but provided a pointed contrast to the 7,500 who attended the previous day's County Championship final. They, and Prince Michael of Kent got a much better game.

The World XV, coached by Bob Dwyer and captained by Philippe Sella staged a magnificent second half rally to overhaul the Tigers. Their performance may have clinched Dwyer's appointment as Director of Rugby at Welford Road next season. If it also gave an idea of the sort of rugby to which Dwyer's new charges must aspire, the English game will already have been done a great service.

Former All Black scrum half Graham Bachop, now playing club rugby in Japan, in action during the Sanyo Cup clash at Twickenham.

Yet to the surprise of those who characterise Leicester as one-dimensional, forward-orientated and boring, the Tigers opened their account with a sensational score, right wing Hackney appearing in midfield and then scorching back to his own wing for a brilliant individual try. When Tarbuck crossed and Liley converted soon after, it seemed we were in for one of those deeply unsatisfying no-contests that often parade as exhibition matches.

That would have suited Leicester just fine. Even though the Sanyo Cup match had been shoe-horned into the calendar between must-win midweek League games against Gloucester and Sale, they did put out their best team at Twickenham. Openly admitting that high on their agenda was the need to avoid injury, Chief Executive Peter Wheeler also expressed the desire to reward players and faithful fans with a good day out.

Bob Dwyer meanwhile had made light of the fact that at Friday's first get-together he had less than half a squad, with the biggest problem sorting out a common language for the players. His confidence that the team would gel quickly seemed misplaced, but not his relish at the prospect of seeing Fijian sevens-mastro Waisale Serevi playing at full back. The little man's brilliant solo try, which he converted himself with a kicking action that could hardly be more economical if it tried, was worth waiting for. Leicester captain Dean Richards restored the advantage in much more prosaic fashion, but a powerful run for a try by French flanker Laurent Cabannes suggested the World XV meant business.

Though Stuart Potter scored again and Liley converted, the game began to change shape and character either side of half-time. Tarbuck's second try, Leicester's fifth, was the final indignity as far as the World XV was concerned. The scratch side's defence at last began to develop some teeth. Jamie Joseph and Graeme Bachop, All Blacks now earning a living in Japan, showed they had lost none of their competitive instincts. Sella, that most uncompromising of centres, sparked off the comeback with a try of his own and as his team grew in cohesion Leicester began to fall apart.

Perhaps they thought the job was done, and they didn't help themselves by throwing on a whole raft of substitutes. The ABC front-row club was broken up as both Richard Cockerill and Graeme Rowntree left the field, and when Dean Richards also retired early it spelled the beginning of the end for the Tigers. The man who had been brought back by England to provide focus, control and massive reassuring presence was even more sorely missed by the team he has epitomised for over a decade. Without him Leicester were far too loose and became unsure how to approach the rest of the game.

As Leicester took their foot off the pedal, the World XV changed gear. The difference between their substitutes and the willing Leicester replacements was that, while both sets of players were keen to seize the big stage, the former were already of proven international quality.

Augustin Pichot, the exciting young Argentinian scrum half reputedly looking for an English club, exuberantly claimed a try to put the World XV in front for the first time, while another replacement, the flying Japanese wing, Matsuda, rounded things off with a score under the posts, forcing Leicester to concede defeat for the first time in twenty-two matches.

Eleven tries in all, and seventy-one points, some great rugby from some of the world's best players, and a sun-drenched afternoon to boot – the organisers could hardly have asked for more. Or could they?

The concept is a good one for the Rugby Union, who need as many pay-days as possible both to cover the costs of rebuilding Twickenham, and to pay the England players. It's a good one for the genuine fans who get the rare chance of a Twickenham day out, and it seems good for the sponsors. The poeple who benefit least from the exercise are the players. Leicester looked tired and lethargic six days later when they lost to Harlequins. They need no reminding that victory in that match would have seen them retain their league title, and so qualify for next year's Sanyo Cup instead of Bath. It's hard to see the west countrymen jeopardising their title in quite the same way, especially in the new professional era.

The World XV already has enough problems in being truly representative for the same reason. If the host team decides not to risk its superstars, the match begins to lose its point. Such are the incredible demands now being placed on players in the southern hemisphere that whenever the match is played it will be difficult to attract the game's really big names. To ensure their English equivalents are all present and correctly motivated, the organisers ought to consider moving the Sanyo Cup to August.

Played then, it could be not only just reward to the Courage champions but a perfect appetiser for the season ahead. Initially the sponsors have a three-year option to renew a concept that on this year's evidence, has genuine appeal. If Bath and their 1998 successors can keep up the momentum, the match could become a permanent part of the rugby calendar. The only thing then left to decide would be which part.

Leicester's Chris Tarbuck takes on the World XV's defence, but it was the scratch squad, led by Philippe Sella (inset) who ran out 40–31 winners.

succeed where competition is fierce

In highly competitive international markets, Pilkington stays ahead manufacturing and marketing flat and safety glass products in over 20 countries around the globe.

SPONSOR OF THE RFU CLUB KNOCKOUT COMPETITION

LOOKING
BACK

THE 1971 LIONS REUNION

BY **BOB McKENZIE**

The living legends arrived like nervous schoolboys at the start of a new term, peering anxiously through the door of the hotel lounge, patting their hair if they had hair to pat and adjusting their ties before joining the early arrivals.

It took only minutes before the stories flowed with the beer, the years fell away and any few doubts about the widsom of a four-day British Lions 1971 reunion tour were swept away.

Soon, 'Merv the Swerve' was complaing to 'Witchdoctor' Smith after hearing of a tactical change in the Lions team twenty-five years ago which no one had mentioned to him.

The 1971 tour party – the beginning of a legend.

It was all mock-serious as they revisited the glories of their New Zealand tour twenty-five years ago, when they became the first British touring team this century to enjoy a Test series success there: won two, lost one, drawn one and unbeaten in twenty-one provincial matches.

The fact that no one had got round to mentioning to Welsh No. 8 Mervyn Davies that the team had adopted a new open-side and blind-side flanker policy in the third Test did not matter because they had won.

That inspired another question from Merv, who wanted to know from tour manager Dr Doug Smith, who became know as 'Witchdoctor' because of his accuracy in forecasting the series results, why Derek Quinnell had not played in the fourth Test.

Had Quinnell not bottled up All Blacks scrum half Sid Going when he came into the side for the vital third game and played the hitherto unrevealed blind-side wing-forward role? 'He was injured – no wonder we told you nothing', growled seventy-one-year-old Smith who then glanced around and announced: 'Ah he was a wonderful No. 8. He did have a great swerve but he could really tackle too.'

Humour was the cement of the friendships, and there was constant laughter as they moved from Cardiff, to a golf pro-am at the Celtic Manor in Newport to a dinner with 1971 Prime Minister Ted Heath in London before a walk-on part at the Middlesex Sevens.

When 'Broon from Troon', alias giant lock Gordon Brown, hove into view outside the golf clubhouse and rapped a putt across the green, John Dawes, that most gifted Welsh centre and Lions captain said from the comfort of his armchair: 'I don't know why forwards try to play golf. It's a game of skill.'

The 1996 reunion – a gathering of the living legends. How many can you recognise? The full caption is on the next page.

Dawes and several others had just been on the course, but when asked what they took at the 12th , the answer was… champagne. Lest this looks a self-indulgent reunion, it should be pointed out that the Wooden Spoon Society was to gain by six figures from this get-together.

The men who made the All Blacks white with rage, red with embarrassment and had Britian singing along to the Beach Boys pop hit 'Sloop John B' refuse to

fade to grey. They survived the rigours of a fourteen-week tour, but could they survive this new strain?

'Your hair was brown when you arrived, Merv', said Dawes, whose girth is sample testimony to the calls of dinners and talks since those halcyon days.

At a dinner in Cardiff City Hall, the years and the weight suddenly fell from them when new-found colour film of their magnificent tour showed the expansive, speedy style of men such as Barry John, Gareth Edwards and JPR Williams as the ball was handled with pace and precision . . . much like New Zealand's 1995 World Cup approach.

Were they the greatest team? The question fuelled many a discussion and Merv, now a forty-nine-year-old sales manager, had the most exciting thought.

'If you matched the 1974 Lions pack from South Africa with the '71 Lions backs, you would have the best', said Merv, who was on both trips.

The '71 Lions were the only British team this century to beat New Zealand in a Test series. They used thirty-three players, including three replacements. Nineteen played in the four Tests, which they won 2–1 with a draw.

THIS IS WHAT THOSE PICTURED ON PAGE 97 ARE DOING TODAY

Back row (left to right):
Gerald Davies, right-wing, 51, rugby correspondent: **Bob Hiller**, full back, 53, schoolmaster: **Mick Hipwell**, back row, 55, jeweller: **Willie John McBride**, lock, 54, retired bank manager: **Roger Arneil**, No. 8, 52, sports leisure clothing: **John Spencer**, centre, 48, recorder at Leeds Crown Court: **Derek Quinnell**, flanker, 46, managing director of water treatment firm: **Mike Roberts**, lock, 50, travel agent: **Geoff Evans**, lock, 53, lecturer: **Alistair Biggar**, winger, 49, insurance broker: **Delme Thomas**, lock, 52, businessman: **John Pullin**, hooker, 54, farmer: **Arthur Lewis**, centre, 54, businessman.

Middle row: **Chico Hopkins**, scrum half, 49 ex-rugby league retired: **Mervyn Davies**, No. 8, 48, sales manager: **Gordon Brown**, lock, 49, building society executive: **John Dawes**, (Captain), centre, 55, coordinator fundraising for rugby clubs: **Dr Doug Smith**, manager, 71, retired doctor: **Gareth Edwards**, scrum half, 49, business consultant: **Sandy Carmichael**, prop, 52, director of plant hire company: **Barry John**, fly half, 51, rugby correspondent.

Front row: **JPR Williams**, full back, 46, consultant surgeon: **Frank Laidlaw**, hooker, 55, director of animal feed manufacturers: **John Taylor**, flanker, 49, rugby correspondent: **David Duckham**, left wing, 49, corporate events organiser.

Not pictured: props **Sean Lynch**, **Ray McLoughlin**, **Stack Stevens** and **Ian McLauchlan**; wing **John Bevan**; flankers **Peter Dixon** and **Fergus Slattery**; centres **Mike Gibson** and **Chris Rea**.

25 YEARS AGO – from the pages of *Rugby World*

SELECTED BY **NIGEL STARMER-SMITH**

January 1972

Since I returned home from New Zealand with the Lions, I have often been asked questions about coaching and coaches. That there seems to be, at long last, a general acceptance of the need for coaching is most encouraging: it won't be necessary, after all, for the would-be coaches of the future to emigrate to New Zealand!

What qualities are necessary in a coach? I would say that the first one is, probably, humility: after all, it is quite an experience for one who was not good enough himself as a player to make a Lions tour to be asked to coach the top thirty players in the British Isles.

Humour, of course, is always necessary – indeed, it is surely a must on a long three-and-a-half months' tour. Firmness too, as long as one is not too dominating and not too concerned about one's image: I dislike the image of the hard man, and it seems to me unfortunate that too many coaches in New Zealand have this kind of image.

A knowledge of technical skills and an appreciation of the tactics of the modern game one takes for granted in any coach, but, above everything else, he must be prepared to listen to other players in a team or squad who may have much to offer.

An interested listener can usually command an attentive audience when he, in turn, has to speak, and after all, communication flows in two directions. Another quality is flexibility.

Before coaching a squad or team, the coach must see clearly in his mind's eye the pattern that he wishes to develop, and everything he does in his training runs, in his coaching sessions, must be geared towards the creation of this ultimate pattern.

Carwyn James, Coach, British Lions 1971

A new slim-line Denzil Williams, the most-capped (thirty-six) Welsh forward, put down his cup of tea in the sitting room of his house high behind the Gwent Valley town of Tredegar and said with a reflective grin: 'The French play hard, you know . . . Their scrummaging is the hardest I have experienced anywhere in the world.'

The giant Welsh prop and British Lion of 1966, now thirty-two years of age, was preparing to leave the next day for Vichy in France, in company with his former Wales and Lions' colleague, Brian Price, who led Newport and Wales with distinction and won only four caps less than Williams. They are enjoying a new

Brian Price and Denzil Williams at numbers two and three in the Vichy line-out.

lease of rugby life with Vichy, the First Division French club, and find the game across the Channel a new challenge.

'We travel to London by car, fly to Paris, and then take the "rapide" to Vichy each Saturday. We play home or away on Sunday and return immediately after the match. Often we fly by small plane to Paris and then by jet to London, and home again by car.

'The games are hard, and we find the atmosphere in the championship matches more tense, even than in Wales. We really enjoy it, but we have to be fitter to survive than we were in Wales!'

J.B.G. Thomas

February 1972

'In my first match for Scotland I was really run off my feet. I had never realised that international rugby was so fast.

'The game today is much better than it was, and the no-kicking-to-touch change in the law has been most revolutionary for the front-five forwards. The tendency now is to encourage more mobile players, where previously there

Wilson Lauder, a Scot who enjoyed his time in South Wales.

were seventeen stones men who really could not run and handle and support.

'Again, this law change has speeded up back-row play by a couple of yards in a 100. It demands a great deal more running in backing-up, getting to the loose ball, and so on – and I certainly feel a shade faster myself.

'Coaching is important, of course, but more important is team spirit, which in the Neath side is wonderful. Without team spirit, even a side of all-stars will not succeed.'

Wilson Lauder, Neath and Scotland

Lauder is right. Team spirit made the Lions into a great side, and team spirit is making the Neath side, under Martyn Davies, a remarkably happy one.

'Luckily, I never panic. That's just me, placid, easy-going. If I'm running five or ten minutes late for training, I don't smash speed limits or go through red lights to get there. I'd sooner be late, and arrive relaxed.

'I'll never switch to league or soccer. The only time I'll play for money is if rugby becomes a professional sport.'

Barry John

The Italian Rugby Federation is looking for a Welshman to act as its coaching organiser – and it is prepared to pay around £200 a month, plus expenses, for the right man.

The offer was made by the new President of the Italian Federation Dr Sergo Conti, when he met Welsh Liaison Officer Mr Elvet Jones, former Chairman of Llanelli, to discuss the future of Wales-Italy rugby relations.

'The Italians were deeply impressed with the Welsh coaching set-up when they made a short tour at the start of the season,' said Jones.

March 1972

Bob Hiller has been quoted as saying: 'It cost some of the Lions £400–£500 to make that trip (to New Zealand). That, in my view, is wrong, and it is time the whole situation was examined and rationalized.'

I do not know how the figure of '£400–£500' is arrived at, but can only assume that, in some cases at least, Hiller is referring to lost wages at home, while the team is away. If so, he is virtually putting in a claim for 'broken time' payments, which caused the original split with the Northern Union, later to become the rugby league. Surely we do not want to start all that over again!

When I was a player on the Lions' tour to South Africa in 1938, it cost me quite a bit. Admittedly, I was single at the time, but had to get four-and-a-half months' leave without pay, from my employers, and had to kit myself out for the trip. That cost about £75, which allowing for inflation, would be nearer £375 today.

I also had to borrow £50 (£250 today?) from various friends and relatives, to help with the 'out-of-pockets', and it took quite a time to pay it all back. While we were on tour we got 3s. (15p) a day allowance – not 75p, as now, though here again inflation probably accounts for the difference.

In the end, however, I thought it was all well worth it. It was a wonderful tour and a great experience. How many youngsters could get a trip like that at such a price? Precious few, I would say.

Vivian Jenkins

The Surrey Schoolboys are enjoying a notably successful season.

Their forward power is impressive, with a formidable pair of locks in NK Gillingham (RGS, Guilford) and N Mantell (Reigate GS) and a skilful hooker and lively worker in N Vinter (Heath Clark GS)

Northern and Gosforth are delighted with the success of the McLoughlin brothers with Ireland, for Ray was a regular member of the Gosforth team when he was studying on Tyneside – indeed, he captained Gosforth – while Feidlam is now living in the area and playing for Northern. He came over from Ireland to see his brother, liked the north-east and settled there.

Jim Renwick, the Hawick centre, became the club's youngest player ever to be capped by Scotland when he was chosen for the recent match against France.

April 1972

John Fidler, the tall policeman and lock who has been one of Cheltenham's leading forwards for several years, recently left the Town club to join Gloucester, though he knows that he faces strong opposition in the Cherry and Whites' ranks from such as Alan Brinn, Nigel Jackson and Jim Jarrett.

Before he could offer himself for selection even in the Gloucester United side, however, Fidler was put out of action in the course of duty. His hand was badly injured in a fracas with an 'undesirable character'.

Watsonians will soon say farewell to their international fly half Ian Robertson. He is teaching at Fettes College, and his coaching duties with the school kept his appearances in club rugby to a minimum prior to Christmas, since when he has turned out fairly regularly.

At the end of the season, however, he goes to London and a post with the BBC.

Before leaving France for New Zealand, All Black scrum half Chris Laidlaw gave me some impressions of French rugby gathered during five months with the Lyons XV, which largely with his help as player and coach, have this season had its best-ever results, with gates seventy-five per cent up on last season's.

When I asked him if he would like to see New Zealand have a club championship like France's, he said: 'Not really. The French competition, for all its virtues, is too serious an affair, and the spirit is often malevolent as a result.'

Brutal play is far more evident in France than in the International Board Countries. In France, the players, the referees and the spectators have considerably less self-control and group-control. Kicking of opponents is common.
Alex Potter

May 1972

Another season is approaching its end, and the familiar cry is being raised about a subject which no one in authority ever seems to tackle successfully. 'Too much rugby' is a constant complaint from players and officials alike, but that, usually, is as far as it goes. No one ever produces the remedy.

That there is too much rugby, in some cases, is all too obvious. Last season, for instance, Gloucester played fifty-one matches and Bristol fifty. In addition, their top players were engaged in the County Championship right up to the final round, and some of them were wanted for England as well.

How many training sessions and weekend 'teach-ins' all this involved is anybody's guess, but in total it must have added up to a vast amount of an amateur games-player's time.
Vivian Jenkins

England's prospects on their short tour of South Africa seem, on the face of it, none too bright. In fact, they could hardly be worse, if one accepts the evidence of the recently-concluded Home International season.

For the first time, the proud wearers of the rose lost all four of their championship matches. Not much to be proud of in that, I fear!

For the first time, too, since 1893–96 Scotland have beaten them four times in succession. That in itself may not have been so bad, but it was the sadly inept display of the England team at Murrayfield that really plunged their supporters into gloom.
Vivian Jenkins

To sum up, the top fifteen schools for the 1971–72 season in my estimation were:
England: Blackpool GS, Downside, Normanton GS, Reigate GS, Rugby and St. Brendan's.
Wales: Bridgend Comp., Caerphilly GS, and Neath GS.
Scotland: Edinburgh Academy, Royal High School and Strathallan.
Northern Ireland: Ballymean Academy, Belfast Royal Academy and Coleraine Academical Institution.
George Abbott

Since his first international match, against Wales on 20 January 1968, Hiller dominated the England sides.

In his nineteen internationals Hiller scored three tries, twelve conversions (out of twenty attempts), thirty-three penalty goals and two dropped goals – 138 points. His colleagues in those nineteen sides mustered between them seventeen tries (one worth four points) and three dropped goals – sixty-one points. No wonder they call Hiller 'Boss'.

In soccer and rugby league there is a World Cup, but not in rugby union. A RU World Cup could

Preparing for the South African tour – England captain John Pullin with props Mike Burton and 'Stack' Stevens.

CATHAY PACIFIC

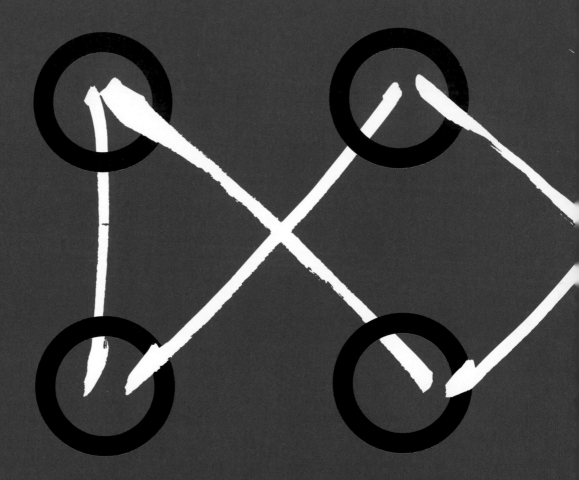

We offer more flights from the UK to Hong Kong than any other airli
China with our sister airline, Dragonair. Cathay Pacific. The Heart o

CONNECTIONS

...as well as the best connections around Asia and also on to 15 cities in
...ia.

be competed for by the five International Championship countries plus Australia, South Africa, New Zealand, Fiji and others – and played for every year.
Reader's letter

June 1972

This, the final of the first rugby union knock-out championship for clubs, was won by Gloucester by two tries, two dropped goals and a penalty goal to a goal, but the match was marred by the sending off of Moseley's international lock Nigel Horton, a policeman, in the fourth minute.

Another British Lion, Llanelli's Derek Quinnell, gave up his job as an electrician to make the 1971 tour of New Zealand. He lost another job when he came home through the miners' strike, and was out of work when he won his first Wales cap against France.

Right Bob Hiller takes his time to land another penalty.

Derek Quinnell comes on as a substitute in the match against France to win his first Welsh cap.

Now Quinnell is back in employment as a representative for a Bath-based firm. 'The publicity given to my plight after the French match did the trick,' he says.

The local publican of a certain inn on the outskirts of Amsterdam was most grateful to Gosford All Blacks whose Easter tour party of twenty-five consumed 600 litres of beer (nearly 1,000 pints) in three days. The publican's normal weekly sale is 350 litres.

July 1972

For fifty years I have been an avid follower of the game, and last season I watched seventy-three matches. I think the award for four points for a try gives a false value. Many teams lose heart after being two goals (twelve points) down, in the early minutes, and eventually get beaten by a huge margin. It would be much better to reduce the penalty goal to two points.

Another great dislike of mine is the long hair of some of the players. It is a handicap to them.
Reader's letter

London Welsh won the Middlesex Sevens at Twickenham on 6 May for the second successive year in one of the most exciting finals for a long

time. It was the sixth occasion they have won the tournament.

The Welsh set off at a cracking pace. By half-time they were leading 18–0 against Public Schools Wanderers, but the Wanderers fought back magnificently and brought the 55,000 crowd to its feet as they cut the lead to 18–14.

Gerald Davies produced a touch of his Lions genius to take the score to 22–14 before the Wanderers made it 22–18. Then they kept up the pressure and were still attacking when the final whistle went to half their challenge.

At Coundon Road recently Bob Hiller was making his usual lengthy preparations for a penalty kick. The Coventry crowd offered the normal helpful suggestions, re- tools and packets of seeds, but one voice, more original than the rest, came up with: 'Take your time – we've got lights!'
Reader's letter

August 1972

Now that the close rugby season is with us, it appears opportune to examine the dangerous drift the game is taking towards professionalism.

We have now accepted national coaches, club coaches, weekend training spells for international sides, advertising on grounds and – last but by no means least – we are toying with the ideal of sponsorship.

All these events are taking place without much comment, and when one sees what the rule of money has done to soccer, and what it is doing to cricket and lawn tennis, then rugby union seems to be the only major amateur sport left.

It is up to all who cherish the principles of this grand game to see that it remains amateur and in amateur hands. To misquote as follows: 'The price of amateur rugby is eternal vigilance.' *F.H. Morgan, Seaford, Sussex*

Top scorers 1971–72
Tries: 40, V Jenkins (Bridgend); 38: JJ Williams (Bridgend); 35: Knight (Bristol); 33: Mathias (Llanelli), Morley (Bristol); 32: Bulpitt (Blackheath), Curling (Aberavon) and Preece (Coventry).
Points: 581: Doble (Moseley); 467: Pearn (Bristol); 415: Stephens (Gloucester); 347: Hill (Llanelli); 342: Page (Bedford); 327: Codd (Rosslyn P); 324: Danile (Newport); 311: Jorden (Blackheath).
Dropped goals: 22: K. James (Newport); 15: G. Davies (Bedford); 13: Phillips (Bath); 8: Nicholls (Bristol).

England's highly successful short tour of South Africa, and their 18–9 win over the Springboks at Johannesburg in the international match, should give them fresh heart for the coming home season.

Their forward play was a revelation, with lock Peter Larter producing the best rugby of his career. John Pullin's captaincy, too, was a vital factor, and the backs, though they did nothing very spectacular in attack, defended magnificently. Sam Doble's goal-kicking on top of all this, put the final seal on his side's success.

The question still has to be asked whether the revival can be carried through to next season's

Five Nations Championship. Scotland, Ireland and Wales have all made big advances in recent years, and England will not need to be reminded of the 32–12 drubbing France handed out to them in Paris last February.
Vivian Jenkins

The article in the May *Rugby World* on the start in Wales of nine-a-side mini-rugby for the Under-11s was interesting, but it is by no means a new idea. The Under-15s in France have been playing eight-a-side rugby for some time, and the French Rugby Federation publishes an eight-page booklet of the rules of the game entitled *Règlement du Rugby Educatif.*

For the past four years, during the Easter holidays, we have taken a team to play matches in France, and last year and this we competed in a tournament at Nantes, with teams in the '*benjamins*' section (this year's qualification being those born in 1959 or 1960) and '*minimes*' section (1957 and 1958).

The basic difference in eight-a-side rugby is that it is played across the pitch, with the five-yard line as the try line, and the touchline as the dead-ball line. There are no posts and, therefore, no conversions. A twenty-five-yard drop-out takes place five yards in front of the goal-line – that is to say, ten yards from the touchline on a normal rugby field. Touchlines are the ten-yard line and goal-line of the fifteen-a-side pitch.
D.G. Ives

Left *Top try-scorer Viv Jenkins of Bridgend.*

Fran Cotton with opponent Norman Mbiko after playing against a South African Bantu XV at Port Elizabeth.

September 1972

'I should like to see the season divided into three parts,' he said 'All the top club rugby, involving championships, etc, should be fitted into the first four months, up to the end of December. Then would come the county matches – on Saturdays – in January and February. Finally, the internationals would take place in March and April, when the county matches were over.'

In this way, he felt, the top player would be called on for only one match a week, at most. Even then, seeing that there are thirty-five Saturdays in the season, he would have plenty on his plate.
Bob Hiller's proposed restructuring of the season

Within a matter of weeks the All Blacks will be in Britain with one major objective – to prove that they have only temporarily vacated the throne of the rugby football world. It would be foolish for players and followers to believe otherwise.

In the light of this tour, the domestic games – i.e., the international championship, the County Championship, the national and county knock-out competitions, not to mention the normal club fixtures – will all be relegated, temporarily at least, to minor roles.

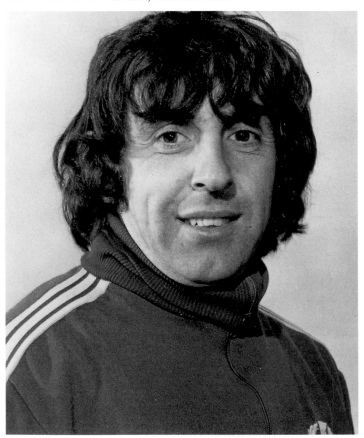

Ian McGeechan, the new captain of Headingley.

This forthcoming season is the crunch for British rugby! There is little doubt that those coaches and selectors now busily preparing for the tasks imposed by the tour are really aware of the enormity of them. Let us hope they are not thwarted by the demands of the domestic season.

Last season we experienced the thrills associated with UK rugby, culminating in the magnificent South African tour by England. Yet all the time there has been the feeling that this was just a pause between the battles against those formidable players from the other side of the world.

The cost (£23,000) of re-roofing the East Stand and of the tours to the Far East and South Africa contributed significantly towards the Union's deficiency of £35,343 in the 1971–72 season.

To meet the additional expenditure of maintaining Twickenham, the price of tickets will go up in the 1972–73 season as follows: stand seats from £1.50 to £2; ring seats from 75p to £1; enclosure from 30p to 60p; ground from 25p to 50p.
RFU AGM

October 72

Gordon Brown, another British Lion, included in his summer routine 6 o'clock in the morning training runs around his Kilmarnock home. During one such run he ran into a wall, breaking a bone in his hand. The state of the wall was not recorded.

The big surprise at the Welsh Rugby Union's meeting was the failure of British Lions' coach Carwyn James to win a seat as a vice-president. He came sixth in a poll in which the five sitting members were re-elected.

James who is to carry on coaching Llanelli, remains in great demand at home and abroad. He was in Nairobi in August on a speaking and coaching engagement.

Headingley, after their worst season for a quarter of a century, have a new captain, new coach and new Chairman of Selectors.

The 1972–73 skipper is Scottish trialist and Yorkshire county back Ian McGeechan, and the coach – the first the club has ever appointed – is one of their former players, Bernard White, now a senior lecturer at Leeds and Carnegie College. An ex-First XV full back Barry Brook has taken over as Chairman of Selectors from Roy Southcott, who has had to give up because of ill-health.

Back in the Yorkshire Cup – for the first time for nearly half a century – Headingley have been exempted until the sixth round, in which they will visit Scarborough on 21 March. If successful, they have a home tie against Halifax in the seventh round.

Ian Kirkpatrick (centre) with New Zealand coach Bob Duff (left) and fellow All Black Keith Murdoch.

November 72

'Kirkie' is still an exceptional player because, at sixteen stones and with considerable pace, he is so damnably hard to check as a runner with the ball.

His try against 'Sid' Dawes's Lions in the second international of last year was undoubtedly one of the greatest in New Zealand Test history. His spin in and out of tackles, his hand-off, his acceleration, his plunge – the Lions simply couldn't cope with him.

He is quiet, retiring, almost excessively modest; but in the few months since the job was thrust upon him, he has grown with it. He now speaks plainly and well and, best of all, briefly. His authority over his players has expanded.

On the field, gathering his men together in a tight little circle, he lets them know exactly what he wants. The respect the players have for him is quite profound. They convey that, however good they may be as congenial persons, 'Kirkie' is just so much better.
TP McLean on NZ Captain 1972–73 tour, Ian Kirkpatrick

The Wallabies tour of New Zealand was a sad chronicle of losses and misfortune, which ended in a humiliating 38–3 defeat by the All Blacks in the third Test. This was the highest score and the biggest victory margin that New Zealand have achieved in a Test.

The New Zealand forwards were so overpowering in the three Tests that they seldom had to, or appeared able to, use their backs consistently or profitably.

Rothmans have emerged with a challenge to *Playfair* on the rugby front, and since this first yearbook of theirs is much bigger in format and number of pages (368 to 160) than *Playfair*, one expects to find it infinitely more comprehensive – which it is. But remember the price differential too – £1.50 to 60p.

December 1972

Don White, the former England coach, once said in an interview, that in an amateur game, which rugby union happily still is, a player's home and job must always come first, and rugby next. If the order is reversed, the effect becomes anti-social. If overdone, it could lead to players leaving the game altogether. Indeed, it is already happening in some cases.
Vivian Jenkins

Romania's first visit to Britian since 1955–56 brought sizeable crowds to Redruth, where they beat Cornwall 18–3 on 7 October; to Devonport Rectory – here the combined talents of Devon and Cornwall lost 3–6 on 11 October; and Torquay, where Devon triumphed 24–23 on 14 October in the best match of the tour.

No stranger to Britain was team manager Viorel Moraru, who played on the previous tour sixteen years ago, together with first coach Teodor Radulescu.

Many of the Rumanians impressed as players who would do well in any rugby company, the 'stars' being skipper and centre Gheorge Dragomirescu, No. 8 Fliron Constantin, wing Gheorge Rascanu and Prof N. Baciu.

Sweet Chariot.

THE CALIBRA FROM VAUXHALL

ON THE LIGHTER SIDE

THE BROKER'S MAN

BY GARETH CHILCOTT

As a rugby player, the nerves, butterflies and tension you suffer before an international or top league game and how you handle them usually depends on how you feel you will play. A truly great player will be nervous and anxious, but will not allow this to hinder his performance. However, that being said, rugby players will usually find themselves in situations on the field that they have trained for and, as rugby is their passion, they are more than able to cope in a frenzy – but imagine the horror. . .

Opening night, mid-December, 2,500 heads in the crowd. Instead of boots, headband and gumshield, you're in tights, corset and full make-up! You are about to go on stage for the first time and spend two and a half hours chasing a girl who has lost her glass slipper! What seemed like a good idea six months ago now seems like a nightmare. I imagined the good money and I thought I would enjoy working with the children, but now the nightmare is upon me!

'Just remember your vital lines,' comes a generous tip from an Aussie who just keeps singing about 'two little boys and Jake the Peg'. It's all right for him, he's done plenty of pantos, this is my first! I've had trouble all week at rehearsals remembering lines – these people just do not speak the same language, e.g., changing rooms are now dressing rooms; a prop is not a front-row forward used to imposing his physical will on an opposite number, but is a six foot rubber tree used for effect; the wings are not the fast, elusive try-scorers, but the sides of the theatre. I have decided that I am completely out of my depth – but what a way to make a living!

Four minutes and counting. Nervously I start to whistle, big mistake, as it's very bad luck to whistle backstage. Apparently it goes back to the days when there were no radio mikes and the instructions to move scenery were delivered by a series of whistling sounds – sixty years earlier I would have had a ten ton Cinderella palace on my head!

'Now, what was my opening line? My god, only two minutes to go and I need the toilet. I can't, no time. How do women cope with tights, you can't do anything quickly! Forget the first ruck and maul, how's my lipstick and rouge? Where's my mirror? I need a mirror! Only one minute to go and I just know I am going to die of embarrassment, everybody will be booing and hissing. Hang on, that is what they are supposed to do. Be positive, Brian Conley is a top performer, he will help me through this, he will adapt to my mistakes, he will see me through this dilemma. Hmm, he has adlibbed all the rehearsals and he will take the piss wickedly. Alas, too late, there's my cue. . .'

'Boys and girls, mums and dads, please let me introduce myself, I am everybody's favourite person the Tax Collector, alias, the brokers' man.' (Hiss, boo). They hate me – great! 'Give the Baron a kicking, Cooch.' Aaagghh a familiar voice – Richard Hill and Jerry Guscott with their families in the front row on the left, just in range for the custard pie scene.

Maybe I am going to enjoy Panto after all. . .

Gareth Chilcott in full panto regalia at the Theatre Royal, Bath.

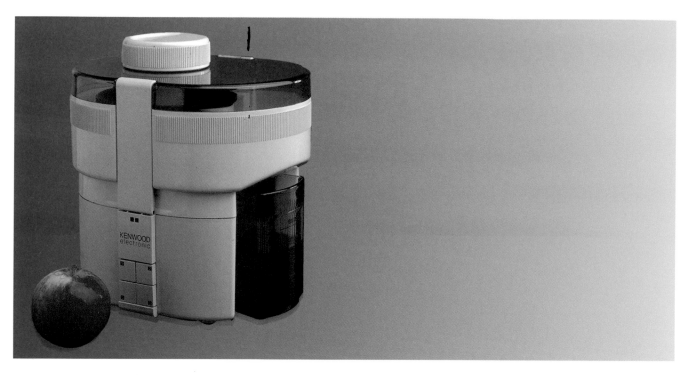

ENGLAND 10   FRANCE 0

Features of the new Kenwood JE600 Juice Extractor	Does our famous French competitor have these?
1 Hi-speed juice extraction at 13,400 rpm.	NON
2 Powerful 250 watt motor.	NON
3 Push-button controls.	NON
4 360° automatic pulp ejection.	NON
5 Extra durable glass reinforced filter.	NON
6 'Power on' safety light.	NON
7 Integrated juice jug.	NON
8 Extra-wide feed tube.	NON
9 1.8 litre pulp container.	NON
10 Made in England.	NON

KENWOOD
JUICE EXTRACTOR

KENWOOD LIMITED, NEW LANE, HAVANT, HANTS PO9 2NH. TELEPHONE: 01705 476000

A TOUR TOO FAR – the rugby writers in Canada

BY **JOHN INVERDALE**

If you are one of those people who firmly subscribe to the view that those who know nothing about sport, usually end up writing about it, stay tuned. You're right.

Some of Britain's finest and most athletic rugby players left this country early in May for demanding tours in far-flung parts of the globe. Purely by coincidence, the Rugby Writers RFC happened to be going to Canada at roughly the same time.

Canada, as you will know, is one of the emerging powers of the world game, looking to clamber their way out of the second division into the élite. The Rugby Writers are members of one of Jacques Cousteau's breakaway organisation, '20,000 Leagues under the Sea'. As yet, their matches are the only ones that Sky has not expressed an interest in televising... ever. As a consequence, the role of the Fixtures Secretary was going to be crucial. A rigorous training session on arrival quickly pinpointed the strengths and weaknesses of the party . . . 'Good job we're only playing a vets game,' said Steve Jones (*Sunday Times*, *Rugby Special*, author, Welshman, Mervyn Davies clone, Chippendale reject).

Now Vancouver is a beautiful place. For fifty-two weeks a year you're never more than two hours away from a ski resort and the harbour doubles up as a working port and a marina. For the outdoor type, when the sun shines, you're close to heaven. For our heroes, those doughty rugby writers more used to downtown seedy bordellos, it proved to be a tour too far.

The Rugby Writers RFC on tour in Canada.

Stuart Barnes appears to be a lone strike force, as the rest of the rugby writers take a breather.

The first fixture was against UCB – *alma mater* of Norm Hadley, and a club where they feed 'em big, and breed 'em big. Their veterans also have better things to do on a balmy Tuesday afternoon in May than pitch up against some has-beens and never-weres who earn their livelihoods slagging off the best in the world for chickening out of tackling Jonah Lomu. These guys have proper jobs, keep the economy moving, employ people and generally live in the real world. They also were under the mistaken impression that the tourists had a few good players in their ranks – 'Put some of the first team out,' they said.

At this point I perhaps ought to say that, mortifyingly, your correspondent here was unable to play in this match owing to a serious injury sustained playing for Esher RFC a month earlier. A broken shoulder and collar-bone confined me to sampling Canadian beer (good), sleeping with Owen Slot of the *Daily Telegraph* (bad) and watching rugby (worse).

So the match kicked off. 'Wasn't that Pat Palmer, the Canadian international running sixty metres to score in the first minute?' I thought so. 'And don't I recognise that prop forward from the World Cup in 1991 . . . and what about that huge bloke in the back row . . . and what about that guy in the centre . . . and what about. . .'

So they had six internationals in their line-up. And we had one. Well, half of one. Stuart Barnes (British Lions, England, Bath, Bristol, Newport, Chablis, Cognac and Cherry B) was a bit unfit. The tour physio, Helen Chesser, the fittest member of the tour party in more ways than one, refused to believe he'd ever been a top international athlete. Barnes put her right. He never had been.

We probably do not need to dwell unduly on the vital statistics of the match. Palmer scored a hatful of tries in the first half and then went back to work. The boys dun OK and fought back stoically. The final margin was not as wide as it might have been, and Helen was up all night treating the injured troops. (I've heard it called some things.)

The hospitality was great, the view from the clubhouse across the harbour, with snow-peaked mountains in the distance, unrivalled. It's for nights like that that you go on tour – may the onset of professionalism never take it away.

But I digress. The next day was a rest day. The tour party split into three. Nigel Botherway, the Mr Big of journalism at Heathrow Airport, organised another of his legendary deep-sea fishing trips. They are legendary because no one ever catches any fish. And so it proved.

Chris Jones of the *Evening Standard* led an expedition into the jungle. It was originally planned as a round of golf, but took on an added dimension when a grizzly bear (big) wandered onto the 17th green and held up play for twenty

The Canadians find it impossible to break through the rock-like defence of the Rugby Writers.

minutes. Chris was just about to play his second shot when he noticed it, but carried on regardless, knowing it would take him that long to get there.

The rest, the adventurous ones, embarked on a white-water rafting expedition in the Rockies. Now as most of you will know, white-water is assessed on a scale from A to F. 'A' is like your jacuzzi... 'F' is like Niagara. This stretch of water was rated at 'E'. We all signed disclaimers before getting in the boat. 'If I die, it's my own fault.' Richard Bath, the editor of *Rugby News* decided this was a licence to kill, and made no effort to rescue one of his colleagues from the *Evening Standard* when he plunged into the frozen river. Stuart Barnes put his own life at risk and hauled him back into the boat – as heroic a gesture as one could imagine – a point Stuart repeatedly made as the night wore on.

After yet another early night, the entire party were up at the crack of dawn for a cycling excursion round Stanley Park, one of the finest city parks in the world, and after a relaxing lunch, set off for the second match of the tour against Scribes RFC. They didn't have any internationals in their line-up, just half a dozen Maoris who made Tuigamala look like a weed.

Well the ethos of the Rugby Writers RFC has always been that it's the taking part and not the winning that counts. It didn't start out as that, but circumstances forced a rethink.

Some of the party went home the day after, to recount tales of crash-tackles and sidesteps and jinks and peels round the front.

Others stayed on to watch the international between Canada and America. I spoke to some of them on their return.

'You wouldn't have believed it,' said one. 'They were so unfit, and you've never seen such poor handling and tackling.'

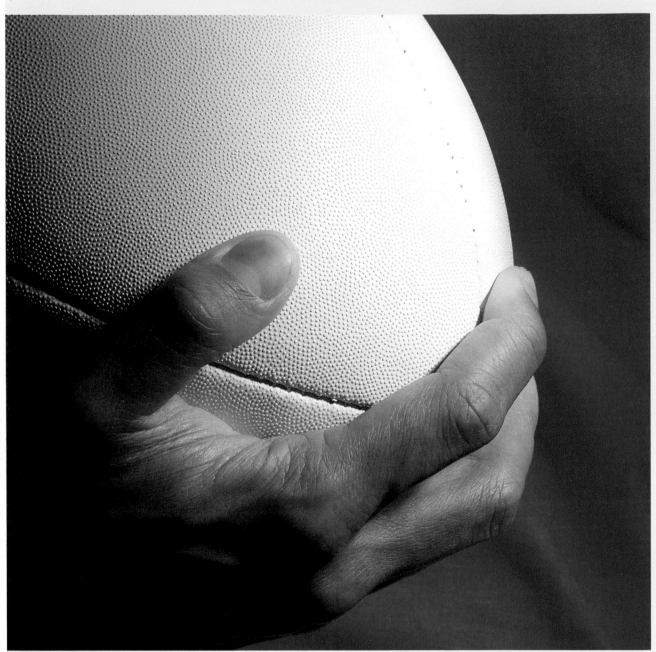

The top players have a number of things in common.

Experience of playing conditions around the world. A capacity to read the game. A sense of teamwork. Strength. Speed. And, above all, the ability to make fast decisions.

HongkongBank

The Hongkong and Shanghai Banking Corporation Limited

Fast decisions. Worldwide.

PREVIEW OF THE SEASON 1996-97

THE FIVE NATIONS CHAMPIONSHIP

BY **BILL McLAREN**

Provided the unseemly row over television cash does not result in England being excluded from the Five Nations Championship, there seems no doubt that England will once more be the team to beat when the 1997 series gets under way on 18 January.

In the last five years England have gathered in three Grand Slams, four outright championships and four Triple Crowns and, whilst there will be the keenest intreest in what style of game they will embrace, they will clearly have the personnel to provide the option of playing it tight, playing it wide or achieving an amalgam of the two.

Of course, England will be under new captaincy this time, with Will Carling having decided to relinquish that responsibility after a magnificent record as England captain of fifty-nine games played, forty-four wins, one draw and only eleven defeats. Whether Lawrence Dallaglio, the Wasps flanker, will inherit the mantle or whether Tim Rodber can rediscover his best form to do so remains to be seen. There are those who would prefer to see Philip de Glanville, the Bath centre, not only given a regular place in the national side, but the captaincy as well.

There could be other changes involving three long-serving stalwarts in the eventide of their international careers. Rory Underwood has had his anxious moments in retreat defence, but his forty-nine tries in eighty-five internationals, placing him second in the all-time list behind David Campese (sixty-four tries in ninety-four), are testimony to his reputation as one of the great strike runners and finishers. But he is now thirty-three and has seen a lot of service. Dean Richards has also passed the thirty-three mark as a veteran of forty-eight caps. He has been the rock on which sundry English successes have been created, not least against Scotland to whom he has proved an object of much frustration. Richards has been associated with a particular pattern of English play and should a more fluent style be sought, he might have to step aside in favour of a greater all-round ability. It certainly will not have been lost on the England management that in the new era of continuity, entertainment is now a key ingredient, as shown by the southern hemisphere countries following the huge success of the Super 12 tournament. New Zealand, for example, now play two open-side flankers and a fast, ball-playing No. 8 as their loose forward trio, Michael Jones, Josh Kronfeld and Zinzan Brooke.

What about Martin Bayfield? The 6ft 10in former police officer has been such a source of line-out ball to England in his thirty-one internationals that it came as something of a shock when he gave way to the Bristol and Army lock Garath Archer for the Scotland and Ireland internationals last season. Archer was reckoned to be a harder type, better suited to the jungle warfare that still passes as line-out play, even under the changed law. The mind boggles, however, at what

Bayfield might achieve in height of jump plus assist under the new ruling which, to all intents and purposes, encourages the noble art of lifting even though it is still is listed as a free-kick offence.

Martin Johnson dominates the line-out as England break Scottish hearts at Murrayfield.

Whether England will pin their faith in forward might and punting half backs, or take on a thoroughly entertaining style of which they are eminently capable, remains to be seen. It certainly was disappointing for the vast England support that in the 1996 championship, which England won on points differential after denying Scotland a Grand Slam at Murrayfield, England actually finished last in the try-scoring list, although they could point to having the best defensive record in conceding only two tries in four games. The try-scoring statistics were:

France: scored 10, conceded 4, differential +6
Scotland: scored 5, conceded 3, differential +2
England: scored 3, conceded 2, differential +1
Wales: scored 6, conceded 9, differential -3
Ireland: scored 6, conceded 12, differential -6

It perhaps also reflected England's style that Paul Grayson scored sixty-four of their seventy-nine points in the championship with seventeen penalty goals, two

conversions and three dropped goals, and also that part of the Twickeham crowd resorted to booing to express their displeasure at Grayson having yet another pot at goal instead of moving the ball by hand.

There is the possibility that the 1997 Five Nations will present a more entertaining image, especially if Scotland and Wales can introduce into their game some of the exciting developments they came across during their recent tours to New Zealand and Australia respectively. They found that the fluency of action and spectacular inter-play that so adorned the Super 12 series had been taken on board by the teams they encountered, especially in the Test series. Although well beaten in each Test, Scotland and Wales had a head start in acclimatising to the new laws which have made the scrummage and line-out more potent areas of initial attack.

Australia beat Wales by 56–25 and 42–3 and by thirteen tries to three, but purely in Five Nations terms, Wales still will be capable of mounting a strong

Above *Paul Grayson (left) and his Northampton colleague Matt Dawson, who formed a new half-back partnership for England.*
Right *Hemi Taylor, who played such an important part in the Welsh win at Lansdowne Road, is stoped by Neil Hogan.*

challenge if they can rediscover the dominant form shown by their forwards in the shock 16–15 victory at Cardiff in March that deprived France of yet another championship. The Welsh try in that match was a brilliant narrow-side effort by Robert Howley, who emerged as one of the new stars of the tournament, a status that he underlined during the tour to Australia.

Certainly the Welsh can be depended upon to seek a fluent game incorporating traditional Welsh handling play in which the power running of Leigh Davies should again be an important element. Wales will be seeking to repeat the kind of scintillating move by which Ieuan Evans scored during the 30–17 defeat at the hands of Ireland in March. Remember how Hemi Taylor provided ignition deep inside his own half and a burst by Leigh Davies and linkage from Jonathan Humphreys and Howley sent Evans scooting home for one of the tries of the championship. There is, too, the educated boot of Neil Jenkins who last season showed his resilience in regaining his cap position from the youthful Bristol

Scottish prop David Hilton celebrates Gregor Townsend's winning try against Wales.

claimant, Arwel Thomas. Jenkins' kicking ability is still very important to Wales. He stands third in the all-time list in average points per match with 11.1 behind Grant Fox (14) and Michael Lynagh (12.6). Wales should also take heart from the victory over France in March which avoided another 'whitewash' and also ended their run of eight consecutive championship defeats.

Although well beaten by the All Blacks to a tune of fourteen tries to five, Scotland played some admirable rugby, especially in the first Test, but they are highly dependent upon Gregor Townsend for creativity and incisiveness and will want to improve their scrummaging so as to have a launch pad for the kind of pivot-five plays that are now on offer under the changed law. There will be an intriguing duel for Scotland's scrum half spot, for Gary Armstrong looked in good nick in New Zealand in the absence of the injured Bryan Redpath, whilst Andrew Nicol showed good form, especially against the Bay of Plenty. There will be a strong challenge to the engine room that faced the All Blacks – Damian Cronin, who will be thirty-four in April, and Doddie Weir – from Stewart Campbell, now with Melrose, and the twenty-year-old Scott Murray, whilst the likes of Brian Renwick, Nick Broughton and Peter Walton will keep the pressure on the loose forward trio of Rob Wainwright, Ian Smith and Eric Peters, even though there are those who believe that Walton could become a top-class international prop. Scotland are intent on going further along the road of the total game by improving their ball retention and delivery, thus keeping the ball alive for intuitive support running.

Ireland finished bottom of the table last season in conceding the most points (106) and most tries (twelve) but they blooded some talented new players, among them the twenty-two-year old Orrell full back Simon Mason and the London Irish fly half David Humphreys, who captained the Irish Schools to a Triple Crown in 1990 and who has brought organisation to Ireland's back play. There also is strong competition for places in the back five as Jeremy Davidson has emerged as a considerable force at lock alongside Gabriel Fulcher, Neil Francis, who will be thirty-three in March, and who still might come to the starting blocks breathing fire and fury with Patrick Johns, David Corkery, Eddie Halvey, Denis McBride, Victor Costello and Anthony Foley to contest the loose forward positions. Ireland also can field a physically impressive midfield with Robert Henderson, the fifteen stones London Irish centre, having already tested the water in the Peace International as partner to the pugnacious Jonathan Bell.

France have won the championship only once in the nineties, which is scant return for such potential, but they have prepared for the 1997 championship with two victories over Argentina in June, and so are well acquainted with the new laws. They were the only ones to beat England last season, but they succumbed to the Scots at Murrayfield and their pack played second fiddle in Cardiff. They even dropped their prolific points-scorer Thierry Lacroix, and seemed unsure as to who was their best scrum half. However, they produced one of the players of the tournament in Thomas Castaignède, whose dropped goal won the game against England and who played both centre and fly half with some of the skill and guile of a Jo Maso in scoring sixty-two points in eight internationals.

England will have the advantage of assessing all of their rivals on the opening day of the series (18 January), when Ireland take on France in Dublin and Scotland entertain Wales at Murrayfield.

Not only could the 1997 series be something of an unpredictable championship, as indeed was that of last season, but if the Five Nations countries want to stay in touch with their southern hemisphere rivals, it would be of benefit if they all tried to play in the same style, in which case they would need some help from the referees. Those who point to the British weather as an excuse for safety-first use of the boot should watch the video of New Zealand's game against Australia in Wellington to open the Tri-Nations tournament and to contest the Bledisloe Cup. Foul conditions but a super contest with some thrilling spread of play as much by hand as by boot!

David Humphreys made an impressive start to his international career.

performance

from

N E X T

KEY PLAYERS 1996–97

BY IAN ROBERTSON

ENGLAND

LAWRENCE DALLAGLIO

MARTIN JOHNSON

After six years with the Wasps club, Lawrence Dallaglio won his first full cap for England against South Africa in November 1995 when he came on a quarter of an hour from the end as a replacement for Tim Rodber. He made an immediate impact and has been first choice in the England back row ever since. He reached the full international side with an impeccable pedigree – he played for England Colts, England Under-21, England Students and England 'A' and not long after his twenty-third birthday he won his first full cap. He played in last season's pre-Christmas international against Western Samoa and then in all matches in the Five Nations, helping England to win the championship. His attributes are all rather obvious. He has the speed to play open-side flanker and reach the breakdown in double-quick time. He has the height, at 6ft 4in, to be a force at the line-out and at 16 and a half stones, he has the power to be a formidable scrummager. He is also good with the ball in his hands and reads the game well. He could be very influential in England's proposed new style of open rugby.

England's success in winning the Five Nations Championship in 1995 and 1996 was largely a team effort, but there is no doubt most of the credit should go to the forwards. The English pack has proved to be the best in the northern hemisphere in recent years and has held its own against most of the top southern hemisphere nations. Certainly, even the All Blacks and Springboks are full of respect for England's line-out play and in particular the outstanding contribution made by Martin Johnson. He is generally regarded as the best front-jumper in international rugby and last season he dominated the club scene for Leicester and the Five Nations for England. At 6ft 7in and almost eighteen stones he has all the physical presence of a great lock forward. He also has an aggressive but disciplined attitude and he is a most effective player in the open. He was the only England forward to play in all six World Cup matches in 1995 and, having played in two Tests for the British Lions in 1993, he is almost certain to be a key member of the 1997 British Lions tour to South Africa.

FRANCE

THOMAS CASTAIGNÈDE

JEAN-LUC SADOURNY

France have had a very talented side during the 1990s, but the one real problem area for them over the past six years has been at half back. They have tried a succession of different scrum halves and fly halves, but have failed to come up with a top-class combination throughout this period. Last season they introduced a new face in twenty-one-year-old Thomas Castaignède and he immediately looked a class apart from previous incumbents like Penaud, Mesnel, Deylaud and Delaigue. Although he plays centre for his club Toulouse, he has all the skills to be an outstanding fly half. He is quick off the mark, has an eye for a gap, instant acceleration, he is elusive and just the player to bring out the best from a wonderful running back division. He can also kick goals and can react under pressure as he showed when he dropped the winning goal in injury time against England in Paris in last season's Five Nations match.

In a curious way just as France have struggled to find a pair of half backs in the past decade, they have been very fortunate to be able to replace one great running full back, Serge Blanco, with another, Jean-Luc Sadourny. Just like Blanco who was fast enough to win twelve caps on the wing, Sadourny also has the speed to play on the wing. He is capable of lightning strikes in the threequarter line and has scored several great tries for France, including two spectacular efforts against the All Blacks. Until the sudden emergence of New Zealand star Christian Cullen in 1996, most critics would have argued that Sadourny and the Springbok André Joubert, were the two best attacking full backs in world rugby. If the French half backs can get their act together, it is likely that, at long last, the French backs can fulfil their huge potential. With wings like Ntamack and Saint-André and an exciting full back in Sadourny, France could start the Five Nations as favourites.

IRELAND

JONATHAN BELL

SIMON GEOGHEGAN

He began his representative career playing full back for Irish Schools in 1992, but quickly showed his remarkable versatility after playing for Ireland Under-21 at centre and on the wing for Ireland on their major tour to Australia in 1994. He hit such good form on that tour that he played in six of the eight games and was chosen at centre threequarter for both the Tests in Sydney and Brisbane. Following that tour he was selected at full back for Ulster in the inter-provincial championship, but he won his next cap on the wing against the USA at Lansdowne Road. Last season he moved from Ballymena to play for Northampton in the Courage Second Division and he helped them win promotion to the First Division. Having played centre and wing for Ireland, he moved to full back against France in 1996 when Jim Staples was injured and it will be fascinating to see where he plays this season. This multi-talented twenty-two-year-old looks equally at home at full back, wing and centre and he has all the necessary skills to play international rugby in any of three positions.

In his first full season of international rugby in 1991, Simon Geoghegan made a dramatic inpact. He scored some spectacular tries for Ireland Under-25, Connacht and Ireland 'B' before winning his first full cap against France. In his first year in the Ireland side he scored memorable tries against Wales, England and Scotland. With the exception of Trevor Ringland, he became the only Irish wing to score three tries in a Five Nations season for a very long time. He is an extremely tenacious tackler in defence. He has safe hands and is a potent mixture of strength, power and pace. The only back in the current Irish team to have played in both the 1991 and 1995 World Cups, he has been first choice for Ireland on the wing for the past six seasons and he is the only Irish back at the moment who looks sure to be in the British Lions team in South Africa in 1997. Still only twenty-seven at the start of this season and with thirty-seven caps to his credit already, he is the established star who can help restore Ireland's fortunes.

SCOTLAND

ROB WAINWRIGHT

BRYAN REDPATH

The first point to be made about Rob Wainwright is his tremendous versatility. He has played in all three positions in the back row and he has played for an amazing variety of clubs. The list includes Cambridge University, London Scottish, Edinburgh Accies, West Hartlepool and Watsonians. He has the height and line-out dexterity to be a No. 8, the speed and ball-handling ability to play open-side flanker and the strength and power to be a blind-side flanker. He won his first cap when he came on as a replacement against Ireland in 1992 and after a full match against France he went on the tour to Australia that year where he played in both Tests. Injuries meant he only played three Tests in the next two years but he re-established his international career in 1995 and has played in seventeen internationals in seventeen months to prove the point. When Gavin Hastings retired after the World Cup in South Africa, Rob took over as captain and he has led Scotland in seven internationals up to the start of this season. A good season with Scotland could see him as captain of the 1997 British Lions.

Initially, Bryan Redpath played his rugby in the south of Scotland in the shadow of Gary Armstrong, but he emerged from that shadow in 1995 to establish himself in the full Scotland side and make himself a genuine contender for the British Lions tour to South Africa in 1997. He has played for Melrose since 1989 when he made his debut as an eighteen-year-old and for most of his club career he has partnered Craig Chalmers. He played for the south of Scotland, Scotland 'B' and Scotland 'A' before he won his first full cap when he came on as a replacement against New Zealand in 1993. In his first ten internationals he played with Craig Chalmers at fly half, but last season he struck up a great partnership for Scotland with Gregor Townsend. He has very quick hands which makes him the ideal scrum half for a back division which wants to run the ball. He is also fully capable of varying his game because he has a blisteringly quick break, he is an excellent support player and he is a good defensive kicker and tackler. Scotland will look to Redpath and Townsend this season to spearhead the attack.

WALES

ROB HOWLEY

LEIGH DAVIES

After representing Wales in Schools, Student and Under-21 levels, he was selected for Wales 'B' in 1993 and then for Wales 'A' in 1994. He went on the full Welsh tour to Zimbabwe and Namibia in 1993, but injury prevented him from playing in the two internationals. At the age of twenty-five he won his first full cap when he played against England in 1996 and he made his mark by not only having a first-class game at scrum half, but also by scoring a try. He went on to play in the rest of the Five Nations Championship and by the end of the season had established himself as not just the best scrum half in Wales but arguably the best scrum half in the northern hemisphere. He has a very fast, accurate service and he is also a tremendous runner in open play. He has brought a new confidence to the Welsh back division and has brought out the best in the Welsh loose forwards. Although he is only embarking on his second season of international rugby he is hot favourite to be the Test scrum half on the British Lions tour to South Africa, and Wales will also be expecting big things from him this season.

At the remarkably young age of nincteen, Leigh Davies won his first full cap for Wales when he played against Italy in January 1996. He made an excellent start to his representative career by making a major contribution to two of the Welsh tries that afternoon and by having a good all-round game. He went on to be first choice for the whole of the Five Nations Championship and he is now an automatic selection in the side. He gained further experience on the Welsh tour to Australia. In his two seasons with Neath he has played mostly in the centre, but he has also played several matches on the wing which underlines his genuine speed and impresssive acceleration. At 6ft and fifteen stones he can add raw power to real pace and he is also a well-balanced, elusive runner with a good eye for the gap and the natural instinct for doing the right thing in the pressure situations. He is exactly the sort of player to inspire a whole back division and, whilst Wales will look forward to heroic exploits from him in the domestic season, the British Lions may well have already pencilled him into their Test team for South Africa.

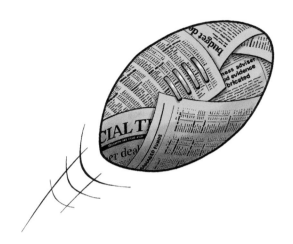

WE ALSO HAVE A PASSION FOR FOOTSIE

We know our way around the FT-SE index and the stock market like others know their way around the rugby pitch. In fact, in the investment field, few are a match for Save & Prosper.

To find out how Save & Prosper can help with your savings and investment plans, call us free on 0800 282 101.

© RFU 1990

THE INVESTMENT HOUSE
SPONSORS OF ENGLISH RUGBY

UNIT TRUSTS · PEPS · PENSIONS · BANKING SERVICES

THE CLUB SCENE

ENGLAND

Change and Change Again

BY BILL MITCHELL

The turning point of the 1995–96 season occurred before a single ball had been kicked in anger, when the IRB declared that the game of rugby union had gone 'open', a move which seemed to take the dignataries of the English game by surprise and resulted in all hell being let loose for the rest of the season.

Any history of the RFU's annus horribilis would go to several volumes, and the issues have been extensively debated earlier in this book. Fortunately, however, there are other things to be said about the season just completed, so we must pass on to those less contentious matters, since there was, in spite of all the stupid distractions, some excellent rugby, much of which was a case of déjà vu, although the emergence of so many wealthy 'sugar daddies' in the English game may well lead to numerous pecking order changes in the near future.

Bath and Leicester remained – and in spite of everything probably will remain – England's best clubs, fighting out the top spot in the Courage League for most of the season, although there was an unexpected climax. Bath seemed to be home and dry and only needed to win their final match at home to Sale to clinch the title, but they lost concentration and had to settle for a draw. This left Leicester, who were playing Harlequins at The Stoop needing a win to overtake them. The prolific goal-kicker John Liley had a kickable penalty in the dying seconds of injury time but missed and the title returned to Somerset.

There was more drama a week later at Twickenham when the pair were again in opposition in the Pilkington Cup final, a dour event which was going the way of the Tigers at 15–9 as the game entered the closing minutes. Bath were attacking in a frenzied manner and were met with a string of penalty awards as Leicester tried everything in their armoury, both legitimate and unlawful, to keep them out. Eventually, referee Steve Lander ran out of patience and bravely awarded Bath a penalty try,

Dismay and disbelief on the faces of the Leicester players as Steve Lander awards the penalty try which decided the Pilkington Cup.

Andy Nicol sets up another attack for Bath against Saracens, who deservedly retained their place at the top level.

which, with a conversion, kept the cup on their sideboard. The dramatics did not end there, however, as the disappointment of the moment was too much for Leicester flanker Neil Back, who appeared to push Mr Lander after he had blown for full-time.

Back came up with an explanation for his action some time after the game, in which he claimed that he mistook the referee for a Bath player whom he wanted to push (was a push something harmless and excusable in any case whoever the target?), and his club earned no credit for supporting his story, which was not accepted by the RFU Disciplinary Committee and Back was handed a ban until the end of October 1996. One can only hope that Back, a fine player, puts this behind him and that other clubs do not follow Leicester's poor example. In this new professional era the last thing we want is a lack of respect for the best interests and image of the game, even though it is now open, and the cynics expect the worst professional excesses to be the norm rather than the exception in future.

The new season will impose many more strains on the top clubs as a result of their participation in the new Euro competitions, and commonsense might have suggested that an increase in the size of Division One would have been the least desirable option, but this is not a time when logic is given any form of priority, as money is the ruler.

So with the all-conquering and excellent Northampton ascending from Division Two, along with London Irish, and bottom Division One clubs Saracens and West Hartlepool being excused from relegation, each team must play a further four league games to add to other routine responsibilities. A case could have been made to exempt Saracens, as they were a good side in spite of their final position, but West Hartlepool, who lost all of their eighteen matches (mostly by huge margins), would probably have benefitted from a season in less eminent company. There is no point in criticising the relevant RFU committee for not enforcing relegation from Division One since they had already sacrificed their own principles by making numerous and confusing changes in the size of leagues elsewhere as a result of demands by certain clubs. Some of these are still subjects to appeal and possible legal action. As a wag once said about the top bosses in another sport: 'Indecision reached!'

This season League Two will consist of a dozen teams and will include the ambitious and well-heeled Richmond, Bedford and Newcastle. Not all can be promoted unless, of course, clubs again decide to move the goalposts and threaten strike action if their demands are not met, having taken a similar position with some success during 1995–96. Anarchy almost reigned then and could do in reality before long. Division Three will number sixteen and Division Four reverts, after only two seasons, to two regional divisions – each of fourteen clubs.

For the record Coventry, a welcome name back from the doldrums, were Division Three champions by a three-point margin from Richmond, and Exeter comfortably won Division Four from the rejuvenated London Welsh. Wharfedale, a new club to vie for honours with the élite, comfortably won the now defunct Division Five North from Worcester, and Lydney, after cruelly missing out on promotion in 1994–95, took the Five South title from Weston-super-Mare, who staged their recovery too late after a moderate start to the season.

The junior scene is no less confusing than that of the senior leagues, with only London retaining their existing system for the new season. The three other divisions – North, Midland and South West – are all about to do 'their own thing' and it will be interesting to judge at the end of the new campaign which reorganisation is the best.

Junior clubs making the move into the senior ranks in 1996–97 include Manchester, once one of the élite, Charlton Park from London's stockbroker belt, Hereford (after a brief spell amongst the juniors) and Newbury, who have a new ground and plenty of ambition. Good luck to them all!

Clubs threatening to break into the big time can number amongst their midst Launceston from East Cornwall, Gloucester Old Boys in South West One, Luctonians, who were the old boys of a now-closed Herefordshire school and seldom lose any kind of match, Southend and Esher from London Division, and Macclesfield from Cheshire. New faces are always welcome to show that even now hard cash and greed are not essential for enjoyable rugby.

Elsewhere, England's various representative sides (in contrast to their dull and restricted national team which scored only three tries in winning the Triple Crown and Championship title) delighted those who were lucky enough to see them in action by their open and enterprising play. The 'A' side was superb, with an excellent fly half in King and the students, although suffering the occasional defeat, were also a joy to watch.

Oxford and Cambridge, who had earlier enjoyed a splendid success against touring Western Samoa, played another fine match at Twickenham with the Oxford fly half David Humphreys scoring all his side's nineteen points in giving an outstanding display. It was a pity that the result should have been settled by a controversial penalty try awarded to the Light Blues by Tony Spreadbury – a forerunner, but probably less justified, to Steve Lander's later decision against Leicester in the Pilkington final.

The BUSA final involved Loughborough and Cardiff Institute at Twickenham, but it was played in dreadful conditions with the Welsh team edging ahead by two penalty goals to one. The Hospitals Cup final was an altogether better game than the previous season with Charing Cross-Westminster holding out against St. Mary's to retain the trophy after the latter had made a courageous second-half recovery.

The services tournament ended in stalemate, each team winning one match. Medicals from Newcastle beat Cornwall's Helston in the Pilkington Shield final and Wigan's rugby league stars won the Middlesex Sevens in style, although in another visit to Twickenham under union laws they were unable to repeat their league rules thrashing of Bath, although it was a memorable day – one that would have been unthinkable until the game went open. Wigan did the good name of their code no harm in the way their players, officials and fans conducted themselves.

Now that barriers have been lowered, one can expect plenty of players to play both codes since the rugby league programme now takes place during the summer months. No doubt we will see a number of exhausted players until they realise that they must make a choice about one code or the other. Before long we may well see top rugby league sides enter the Pilkington Cup and other union competitions. Why not?

The possibility that the satellite television companies might also force a merger between the two codes cannot be ruled out. After all, they plan to meet most of the bills and will RFU officials be able to resist demands for change in this and other directions?

We still await the first former league player to appear for a union international side – Jonathan Davies may be too old to play for Wales again – but it is bound to happen soon and few will regret that.

Russell Earnshaw (7) jumps for joy as Cambridge celebrate Jonathan Evans' decisive try against Oxford at Twickenham.

IRELAND

The Year of Uncertainty: Mark Two

BY **SEAN DIFFLEY**

Last year in these honourable pages we labelled the season as 'The Year of Uncertainty'. It will hardly cause too much eyebrow-raising that this season's title should read: 'The Year of Uncertainty – Mark Two.' In fact even the close-season developments suggest that the 1996–97 season will be uncertain with knobs-on.

For a start, the new professionalism and the liberal financial offerings dangled by the clubs in England means that the 1996–97 season will start with only two of the Irish side that played at Twickenham last season still in Ireland, with Irish clubs. They are flanker Denis McBride and centre Maurice Field. Otherwise the trek has been to pastures new. The great fear in Irish rugby now is that the game, a high-profile one in Ireland despite the comparatively low rugby population, will descend into something like domestic football which has a very low status on the island of Ireland. The situation is that Irish children follow English football, can name all the players of Manchester United or Liverpool or Arsenal but would probably be incapable of naming or recognising a local player.

At the mid-summer IRFU annual meeting in Dublin the opinion was that it would take a few years for 'matters to sort themselves out'. This was certainly the opinion of Syd Millar and Tom Kiernan, the two Irish International Board representatives who had attended the historic meeting of the International Board in Paris which had ushered the game into its new era. The general view among the members of the IRFU was that realism would take a while to reassert, and that the code should patiently await the return of commonsense. In short, that Irish rugby should reconcile itself, patiently, to several years of uncertainty.

It was a difficult summer for international team manager Pat Whelan and his fellow selectors Donal Lenihan, Frank Sowman and Joe Miles. Amateurs all, giving their time like rugby-people of a former era, they had planned rigid strength-training programmes for the squad under their professional coach Murray Kidd. The obvious deficiency among Ireland's leading players, was a lack of upper-body strength. But Whelan and his 'wild-eyed idealists' got a severe shock when they converged on the Irish Army's training terrain on the Curragh. The players had sent their agent to inform Mr Whelan and his cohorts that they 'were not prepared to train until the insurance issue was resolved'.

So the sessions had to be called off and the firm financial offers to the players, which had been ready in contract form for ages, remained unsigned. The resultant hubbub made it clear that the players were very far removed from being popular with the Irish rugby public.

They had originally been offered £25,000, a car, plus £3,000 per international match and a £1,000 win bonus. When the insurance issue arose the £25,000 was increased to £30,000 with the players left to arrange their own insurance which was estimated to be £800 each. And, of course, there was money too for squad training.

Recent results, especially the pathetic resistance to the scratch Barbarians side

Above *Phil de Glanville is pursued by Jeremy Davidson in the Peace International at Lansdowne Road.* Right *St Mary's create a temporary hold-up for Shannon who went on to win the All Ireland League for a second successive year.*

in the Peace International at Lansdowne Road, had left a rather sour taste among rugby followers and the wheeling and dealing, plus the intrusion of an agent, made rugby fans wonder if the players would ever begin to earn the money they so ardently canvassed. Certainly the arrival of the professional era did not show the Irish squad in its most attractive light.

So, as we entered the new season the best players had departed for England and that was clearly going to affect standards at home. Shannon won the Insurance Corporation All Ireland League for the second successive year and, as usual, Division One was dominated by Munster clubs. Overall, it was the least satisfactory All Ireland in that the season had been broken into two sessions with the result that interest waned. It was agreed that the experiment, introduced at the behest of the clubs, had not been a good one. So for this season the formula will be much as it used to be; taking into account club, inter-provincial and national team requirements.

Due to this restructuring, there was no relegation from Division One and three clubs were promoted; Old Crescent, Dungannon and Terenure College. The promotion of Old Crescent means that there are now four Division One clubs from Limerick; Old Crescent, Shannon, Garryowen and Young Munster. Quite a tribute to the strength of the club scene there.

Further extending the League is the addition of the junior provincial league winners, Ballynahinch (Ulster), Suttonians (Leinster), Creggs (Connacht) and Richmond (Munster) who will feature in Division Four this season.

At inter-provincial level the successful side was Leinster. They won their matches against Ulster, Munster, Connacht and the Exiles impressively, ending a decade of failure to become champions and to manage an average of thirty-four points per match.

They also did well in the highly entertaining Heineken Cup, beating Milan and Pontypridd in two closely fought and exciting games. They were beaten 30–14 by Cardiff in the semi-final. Irish rugby was delighted with the competition and the Irish are enthusiastic supporters of the concept, won by Toulouse who beat Cardiff in the final. Ulster also took part but lost to Cardiff at Bègles-Bordeaux.

David Tweed of Ulster climbs high in the line-out against Leinster in the Inter-Provincial Championship.

The more pleasant face of Irish rugby is at under-age level where last season was a triumphant procession by the Under-21 side, the Irish Schools and the Ireland 'A' side.

Once again the Schools took the Triple Crown, beating Scotland 37–12, England 12–9 and a week later took the third scalp by beating Wales 13–12. The Under-21 side beat England 23–10, Scotland 21–9 and Wales 20–12. And even if the 'A' side was overwhelmed by England at Richmond, it did beat Scotland 26–19 and Wales 25–11. All of which underlined again, as the IRFU have been claiming, that the structure of Irish rugby is basically strong and that there is talent out there.

The problem for Pat Whelan, Murray Kidd and company is to translate it all into a meaningful side at full international level. That should not be impossisble if they can focus the players' minds on building themselves up in preparation to taking on the big boys – instead of concerning themselves with insurance.

Imagine Willie Duggan, Fergus Slattery or Willie John McBride discussing insurance! It's the uncertain times we live in.

SCOTLAND

Cup Fever and the Green Machine

BY BILL McLAREN

Whilst things are just not the same for Scotland's clubs in the first full season under the professional banner, one thing that has not changed is the ambition of all of their rivals in the SRU Tennents Premiership to topple Melrose from the title perch they have occupied in five of the last seven seasons.

That Melrose ascendancy, since 1990, has been interrupted only by Boroughmuir (1991) and Stirling County (1995). Whilst Melrose gathered in the 1996 title on points difference, there seems no doubt that they will start the new season as the team to beat, especially now they have taken full advantage of the new era of professionalism to safeguard their status by reaching out to attract more class players to the Greenyards.

Of course, they would not have won the 1996 championship had Stirling County been able to fashion a forty-three points margin of victory over Heriot's FP at Goldenacre in the closing fixture. Stirling, in fact, won by only 34–14, so that although Melrose clinched the title, Stirling could take satisfaction in the fact that in home and away fixtures with Melrose, they took three points out of a possible four.

Since then, however, there have been changes. Melrose have lost their thirty-nine-times capped back five forward Doddie Weir to the moneyed Newcastle, and their fleet-footed wing Craig Joiner to Leicester. At the same time Melrose have recruited strongly. International prop Peter Wright has been enticed away from Boroughmuir and in the process became the first Scottish player to engage a professional business adviser to oversee his contract conditions. Stewart Campbell (thirteen caps) has switched to Melrose from Dundee High School FP, clearly with a view to compensate for the loss of Weir, who has been such a prolific source of line-out ball to the Melrose club throughout their championship seasons. To fill the gap left by Joiner, Melrose have recruited two of the quickest strike-runners in the Scottish game, Derek Stark of Boroughmuir, five-times capped and top try-scorer with six on Scotland's recent tour of New Zealand, and Mark Moncrieff of Gala who played in all five non-cap Tests during Scotland's tours to North America in 1991 and the South Pacific in 1993. That isn't all. That gifted, tricky little artiste, Scott Nichol of Selkirk, has taken the route to the Greenyards, so that Melrose are now able to field a back division containing six capped men; Rowen Shepherd, Stark, Graham Shiel, Nichol, Moncrieff, Craig Chalmers and Bryan Redpath. Such recruitments have not made Melrose exactly flavour of the month with rivals who have lost quality men, nor indeed with some of their own. One possible loss was that of Gary Parker, who might well have moved up the road to play for Gala in the Second Division. Parker, a former Scottish Schools international who has played international football for New Zealand, has achieved some notable scoring feats in the Melrose jersey as a tricky runner and a goal-kicker who always seeks to do the ball a fearful injury. He is, too, a cheery personality who, after much deliberation, decided to stay at the

Greenyards. Incidentally, Gala's former coach, Peter Dods, will be guiding the fortunes of Stirling County this season.

The Premier Division will not quite be the same without Gala and Edinburgh Academicals who have been hit by the decision of their international loose forward David McIvor, to return to his roots at Glenrothes who joined the premiership having won Division One of the National Leagues. It will be difficult for Edinburgh to replace the inspirational McIvor who, through his ball-winning and tackling, put his body on the line every Saturday.

Stirling County, with their three internationals Kenny Logan, Ian Jardine and Kevin McKenzie, are always liable to mount a a strong championship challenge. As indeed are Watsonians, who are so often there or thereabouts as the nearly men of the Scottish game. It would surely round off the

Doddie Weir on the burst against Gala – Melrose will have to find a replacement for their 1996–97 campaign.

illustrious career of Gavin Hastings if he could be part of a championship winning effort by Watsonians after his sojourn in American football with the Highland Claymores. His brother, Scott, who became Scotland's most capped player with sixty-two, one more than Gavin, in the second Test against New Zealand, is confident of having at least two more seasons in the top flight and with these two in harness, Watsonians are capable of toppling any of their rivals. In Tom Smith, the club also has a mobile prop who came close to a cap in New Zealand and who will be a wiser player following that tour. Another key figure has to be fly half Duncan Hodge, whose two dropped goals gave Scotland 'A' their 17–15 win over the touring Springboks in 1994, and who is rapidly gaining status as a genuine cap challenger.

Boroughmuir have been hurt by the loss of Stark and Wright, but are always a force to be reckoned with. Elsewhere the Goldenacre faithful have been looking for a Heriot's FP revival, with the retired British Lion Ken Milne now involved with their coaching. It also would give much pleasure to the Goldenacre support if Cameron Glasgow would overcome past disappointments by following his famous father, Ron, into cap status.

Rivetted interest also has been directed towards the challenge from Wansfield Park, the current resting place of the SRU Tennents Scottish Cup, which Hawick won against all the odds. Such an achievement hardly seemed likely when Hawick finished fifth in the eight-team premiership, with seven defeats from fourteen games. Curiously Hawick had risen to the occasion against the heavyweights with two wins over Stirling County and one each against Melrose and Boroughmuir whilst losing twice to Heriot's FP and once to Gala.

In the cup, however, Hawick revived memories of halcyon times as they struck a blow for home-grown talent. Before a rivetted audience of over 4,000 at neutral Netherdale in the semi-final, Hawick outplayed the champions Melrose, despite conceding a try to international centre Graham Shiel within one minute of the start, then an ninety-metre intercept try by Derek Bain that restored the Melrose lead to 15–12 midway through the second-half. The crucial score, however, was by Hawick's twenty-year-old full back Colin Turnball. When Chalmers failed to find touch, Turnball weaved his way through the seemingly impregnable Melrose defence for an astonishing try. That, plus twenty-three points (six penalty goals, one dropped goal and one conversion) from the Scotland 'A' fly half Scott Welsh, son of Rob, capped against Ireland and England in 1967, gave Hawick a notable triumph that dashed Melrose's aspirations of a premiership and cup double.

What made their cup defeat of Melrose all the more memorable, was that Melrose had given the performance of the cup series with a magical display of power, inter-play and continuity in their 50–22 quarter-final victory over Boroughmuir. That had been a vintage Melrose display, seemingly marking them out as invincible.

Good times return to Hawick – Brian Renwick holds aloft the Tennents Cup.

Watsonians were still the favourites for the final. They had already beaten Hawick twice in the premiership, 33–17 and 39–6, and in their cup run they had amassed 273 points to twenty-five, thirty-five tries to three, in beating Edinburgh Academicals (33–6), Stewarty (62–3), Langhelm (98–3), Heriot's FP (23–6) and Dundee High School FP (57–7). When they shot into a 15–0 lead after only eighteen minutes of the final, inspired by a brilliant try from Scott Hastings, a runaway score seemed possible. But with their captain Brian Renwick at the heart of a revived pack effort, and another cracking try from full back Turnball, Hawick ground their way back to 15–12 down with seven minutes to play. Whereupon Hawick and Welsh exploited a tap penalty resulting in a try by Welsh and a victory for Hawick by 17–15.

For Watsonians it was another case of so near and yet so far. They are a club that deserve success for the highly attractive style of play that they have always adopted. As for the Hawick players, there was the huge satisfaction of having emerged from the shadow of their illustrious predecessors who had been Division One champions on ten occasins. The 'Green Machine' as they were dubbed by their overjoyed supporters, had taken their own Hawick Saxhorn Band to the Murrayfiled final, and the Drums and Pipes Band provided inspiring musical accompaniment throughout the game. The huge Hawick forty-times capped, double British Lion Hugh McLeod, admitted to having leapt to his feet and thrown his

arms in the air for the first time in his life, when Welsh scored the clinching try. On their return home, the Hawick squad, their officials and their coach Billy Murray, the former Scotland 'B' flanker, were given a rousing reception from 8,000 of their townspeople as their open deck bus did a parade of the High Street. One person missing was Jim Renwick, Hawick's fifty-two-times capped British Lion, who had arranged a family holiday overseas, yet his work as coach of the Hawick backs had been an integral part of their successful adoption of an entertaining style of play that suited their personnel and evoked memories of great times in the past in which Renwick himself had been a key figure.

The SRU and their sponsors, Tennents, deserve high credit for the massive success of the competition. The less fashionable clubs had their chance to take on the giants, and a crowd of 22,709 turned up at Murrayfield to enjoy a touch of festival on the back pitches as well as the Bowl, Shield and Cup Finals. There were pipe bands, jazz bands, celebrity relays, craft and merchandise stalls, face painters and picnic areas. There were beer tents too! It was a great day out, culminating in three cracking finals from which the winners were Edinburgh Academicals (who beat Selkirk), Currie (who beat a sadly understrength Stirling County) and Hawick. Cup-tie rugby is here to say in Scotland.

Delight on the faces of the men in green as Scott Welsh scores the try that won the cup for Hawick.

WALES

Suddenly Everything Went Daft

BY **DAVID STEWART**

For Welsh rugby 1995–96, and the close season which followed, were like Clapham Junction. All change. The old game had rumbled on for more than 100 years in a format which altered slowly, when at all. Then suddenly, everything, and nearly everybody, went daft.

And to think a Welshman started it all! In the funereal atmosphere of the IRFB press conference at a Paris hotel in August 1995, Vernon Pugh QC, Chairman both of his home union and the International Board, announced that with immediate effect rugby union would be 'open'. And 'open' is what the borders of Wales have truly become. To continue the transportation metaphor, the summer of '96 has seen the best in the west hop into their sponsored cars, take advantage of the second Severn crossing and disappear up the M4 to the big city. If not milk and honey, then certainly money – some large dollops of it too.

As the cheque book and contract era takes shape, only Cardiff, backed by millionaire businessman Peter Thomas, appear to have the funds and the structure in place quickly enough to sign up the best talent currently available, and accordingly remain competitive in a UK, and now European, context. And the capital's club needed to do something. Beaten at Stradey Park in the cup, and deservedly pipped by Neath for the league title, they were trophy-less as well as Alex Evans-less by the season's end. There was little doubting the impact of the Aussie's departure upon their playing style and performance. As Evans left another big name came in. Few are bigger than the Pied Piper, Jonathan Davies, who became the first returnee from the other professional code, after some protracted transfer negotiations. His 1995 financial package, initially attractive in the early days of the professional game, would be rapidly overtaken as the financiers and property developers started adopting London clubs later in the season.

Davies eased himself in. In truth he played little real rugby, then spent the summer preparing to be unleashed as part of a half-back unit with Robert Howley, which the pair hope to take all the way to the first British Lions Test in Cape Town next June. In addition to Howley, the best player in Wales last season, the Blue and Blacks have signed most of the good young talent in the Welsh team including Leigh Davies from Neath, Justin Thomas and medical student Gwyn Jones from Llanelli, plus David Young from Salford. One unfortunate side effect is the departure of supporters' favourite Mike Rayer – one of a decreasing number actually born and brought up in the city – to the hot-bed of rugby that is Bedford. Nigel Walker nearly followed him, but will remain at the club with an increased role as fitness coach. It is surprising that the Welsh selectors apparently see no future for this man at top level. On a sunny night in early May at Pontypridd, as Cardiff clung desperately to their Heineken League challenge, he scored a length of the field try which, for individual brilliance, ranks with those scored by Christian Cullen in the Hong Kong Sevens or Matt Burke against New Zealand.

The Heineken League experimented with a system of bonus points awarded for tries scored. As a result, although Neath lost one more game than Cardiff, the Welsh All Blacks triumphed by the narrowest of margins a matter of days after they had been vanquished by Pontypridd in the SWALEC Cup final. They reversed that result on a gloriously warm final league Saturday at the Gnoll. Time was running out fast when No. 8 Steve Williams, the most improved player in the land, summoned a final effort from heaving lungs to get in at the corner. Joy unbounded for coach Darryl Jones and his youthful side, many of whom he had developed a couple of years earlier at Neath Tertiary College. Alas it could just be the last time such good times roll at the Gnoll. The exciting young half backs Paul Williams and Patrick Horgan will stay, as will the most promising hooker in Wales Barry Williams, but as well as Leigh Davies, the brothers Llewellyn have gone. The pair, trusted servants together in the boiler house throughout the 90s, will be playing their club rugby in front of Harlequins supporters, better heeled and more genteel than those whose chants of 'Neath, Neath, Neath . . .' have curdled the blood of many a visiting player. Ignore what any Cardiff supporter may tell you – the pace, dash and daring of Neath's young side made them worthy champions.

Robin Jones of Neath leads the charge against Pontypridd in the SWALEC Cup final.

A great moment for Nigel Bezani.

As were Pontypridd in the cup. This was the real fairy story of the year. Yes, they won Whitbread and Western Mail merit tables back in the 70s, but this was the first real trophy won by the club representing the town which is the gateway to the Rhondda Valleys. Their achievement was a genuine team effort, but four people, in particular, were crucial. Three were coach Dennis John, his son Paul, an effective scrum half and tactical leader, who in turn served Neil Jenkins, now the holder of just about every significant point-scoring record going. The greatest pride though was displayed by the daddy of them all, prop-forward Nigel Bezani. In the shadow of his fortieth year, this descendant of Italian immigrants, a self-confessed 'bad boy made good' (as happy in motor-cycle leathers as in shorts and jersey) has put body and soul into his four-year term as captain. His heritage betrayed him when the tears flowed freely as he clutched the SWALEC Cup at the National Stadium, days before smiling his way into retirement, and a place on Pontypridd's management team. The game itself was a cracker, which when set beside the bore that was Bath versus Leicester at Twickenham, restored some much needed optimism to the Welsh game.

What of the other leading sides? Llanelli are a special club in many ways, with some fairly special people. Gareth Jenkins was restored to their coaching ranks, but they lost Alun Lewis to the Welsh set up. As in the past they lost players to the North – except this time Colin Stephens and Phil Davies have ended up at Leeds rugby union club, not their thirteen-man equivalent. There was a happy night in November when the club honoured favourite son Ieuan Evans with the first testimonial match of its type for a player in this country. The man's standing in world rugby was marked by the presence of the like of Jonah Lomu, Sean Fitzpatrick, Jason Little, Gavin and Scott Hastings and a host of others. Truly, only players of special character could make it back to the top level after the sort of hideous leg-break he suffered the previous year. In competitive rugby, it did not really happen for the Scarlets last season. July, however, has seen an influx of some money, and with it some of the better younger Welsh forwards who toured Australia.

Up the road Swansea had one of their Jekell and Hyde years. Virtually invincible at St. Helens but hardly knowing how to win away from home. The prodigal Gibbs has returned from rugby league. Little Arwel Thomas (like Scott and Jonathan, another one developed by Neath who then moved on) returned from Bristol, and probably waved to Robert Jones going the other way on the M4. The irony of the scrum half is that he will now link up again with Alan Davies, the former Welsh coach who felt able to do without his subtle skills for much of his time in charge of the international team.

As for the rest Bridgend, Newport and Newbridge occupied their regular mid-table slots, and spent the summer watching their better players disappear elsewhere, respectively Howley to Cardiff, Voyle and Gibbs, A to Llanelli. Mind you it is not easy to keep up. Gareth Thomas announced at the season's end that he was going to join his mate Neil Jenkins at Pontypridd only to return from the Australian tour saying he was staying at Bridgend after all. One player definitely on the move, again from the Gnoll, but this time without any hard feelings is former Welsh captain Paul Thorburn. Determined to show that his appointment as Tournament Director for the 1999 World Cup does not mean he is decrepit just yet, the full back, after many years in the black of Neath, is joining Dunvant once again promoted from Division Two.

What happens next? I daren't tell you the plans, because by the time we go to print, they will probably all have changed. Terry Cobner, Director of Rugby at the WRU, wanted district teams representing Wales in the 1996–97 Heineken Cup, yet the initial draw has Pontypridd, Llanelli, Neath and Cardiff in the four pools. Neath and Pontypridd, as league and cup winners, had arranged to play Bath and Leicester their English counterparts in a high-profile curtain raiser to the new season – before the RFU (when will they start calling it the English RFU?) stepped in to cancel. Pontypridd threatened legal action for breach of contract; the RFU were responding to similar threats from Orrell who stood to lose a lucrative early-season fixture against Bath.

Is this the future for the old game? This article goes to publication as the Atlanta Olympics are concluding. 128 nations have taken part. Until recently the development of Italy, Romania, Canada, the USA and several Pacific islands suggested a raising of standards in rugby worldwide. In the new moneyed era most of those now seem likely to regress. Will they be the only ones? Do Wales and their Celtic cousins face similar hazards? Thus the significance of the Five (or Four) Nations, with all the kerfuffle over the sale of television rights, comes sharply into focus. That topic is much discussed elsewhere in this book. Suffice to say that English followers of the game can have little comprehension of the incandescent fury of their opposite numbers in Wales, Scotland and Ireland at the perceived betrayal perpetrated by Mr Hallett and his committee for an additional thirty pieces of silver. The rest of us pin our faith, negotiation wise, in the aforementioned Mr Pugh. May he preserve what was the best of the old order in this ever-changing world.

FRANCE

L'Argent and Money

BY **CHRIS THAU**

As far as the French are concerned, the change from amateurism to professionalism did not have much of an impact. One could argue that it was business as usual – in other words, money changed hands, players got paid, clubs demanded and got transfer fees, France nearly won the Five Nations and Toulouse won the championship. This was Stade Toulousain's third Bouclier de Brennus in a row, a feat achieved previously by Stade Français in the nineteenth century, by Toulouse in the twenties and Lourdes in the fifties. Toulouse, though, is the first to achieve the treble twice and now have their eyes firmly set on SBUC's (Bordeaux University) seemingly unbeatable record of four titles in a row, 1904–1907.

The match against Brive, still without a championship title in their trophy room after four finals, was full of drama and graft, but painfully short of class and style. Those who had hoped for rugby champagne, or at least for a good and subtle Burgundy were cruelly disappointed. It was a full-bodied country wine, without nose, dash or romance. It was strong and colourful yet made for a carafe rather than a cellar.

It needs more than one Brive defender to halt the progress of Toulouse prop Christian Califano.

The Toulouse pack, with their front row Claude Portolan (in his farewell game) Soula and Califano to the fore, dominated the proceedings and kept a tight grip on the game. The two opposing international fly halves, Christophe Deylaud and Alain Penaud, seemed strangely i n a r t i c u l a t e , overwhelmed by the occasion. Brive scored an unlikely try in injury time before the half-time break, but Toulouse restored the balance with a touch-down a quarter of an hour before the end.

A third successive championship for Toulouse.

Trying to sum up the feeling in the aftermath of the game a French newspaper gave the match report the following headline: Toulouse v Brive – two tries and eight penalties.

It was Toulouse's thirteenth success in seventeen finals. They left the mighty Béziers behind with eleven titles out of fifteen appearances in the final. Castres, won the reserve final 18–13 and more significantly defeated Toulouse juniors 21–13 in the Under-19 final played as a curtain raiser to the big match. The ladies from Chilly-Mazarin beat Romagnat 3–0 to win the women's title.

Professionalism will eventually leave its mark on French rugby. So far no club owners in the mould of Nigel Wray or Sir John Hall have emerged. The market did not go berserk and the players kept their cool. The clubs tried to flex their muscles, but the Fédération remained firmly in control. Unlike England and Wales, in France the sporting scene is regulated by government decree and the FFR is the sole organisation authorised to run rugby union.

The players who felt that they could make a bit more (in some cases a lot more) money abroad signed for English clubs; Sella, Benezech and Cabannes are the earliest to cross *la Manche*, opting for money rather than *l'argent*. This process is likely to accelerate, unless the home unions take protectionist measures similar to the FFR. After their lucrative *séjour* in Durban, when they played for Natal in the final stages of the Currie Cup, Olivier Roumat and Thierry Lacroix told their peers that there was a lot of money to be made in South Africa. However, their autumn ban and the firm attitude of the FFR, allied with the swift decisions of the IRFB who made it virtually impossible for globetrotting mercenaries to move from place to place in search of 'rugby gold', deterred further French players from following the South African route.

FIXTURES 1996–97

OCTOBER 1996

Tue, 1st — Heineken League Div 2
Sat, 5th — ITALY v WALES
Courage Leagues 1,2,3,4N,4S
SRU Tennents Premiership 1/4
SRU Tennents Nat Leagues 1/7
Heineken League Divs 2/5
Irish Inter-provincial Championship:
  Munster v Ulster
  Leinster v Connacht
Tue, 8th — Newport v Barbarians
Sat, 12th — Heineken Cup (Europe):
  Bath v Edinburgh
  Pontypridd v Benetton Treviso
  Llanelli v Leinster
  Pau v South of Scotland
  Brive v Neath
  Munster v Milan
  Wasps v Cardiff
European Conference all pools
Pilkington Cup Round 2
Courage Leagues 2,3
SRU Tennents Nat Leagues 1/7
Heineken League Divs 2/5
Sun, 13th — Heineken Cup (Europe):
  North & Midlands v Ulster
Tue, 15th — Heineken League Div 2
Wed, 16th — Heineken Cup (Europe):
  Benetton Treviso v Dax
  Edinburgh v Pontypridd
  Leinster v Leicester
  South of Scotland v Llanelli
  Ulster v Harlequins
  Neath v North & Midlands
  Milan v Toulouse
  Cardiff v Munster
European Conference all pools
Sat, 19th — ITALY v AUSTRALIA
Heineken Cup (Europe):
  Dax v Edinburgh
  Pontypridd v Bath
  Leicester v South of Scotland
  Llanelli v Pau
  Harlequins v Neath
  Munster v Wasps
  Toulouse v Cardiff
European Conference all pools
Courage Leagues 2,3,4N,4S
SRU Tennents Nat Leagues 1/7
Heineken League Divs 2/4
SWALEC Cup 3rd Round
Heineken Cup (Europe):
  North & Midlands v Brive
Wed, 23rd — ITALY v AUSTRALIA
Sat, 26th — Heineken Cup (Europe):
  Bath v Dax

Edinburgh v Benetton Treviso
Pau v Leicester
South of Scotland v Leinster
Brive v Harlequins
Neath v Ulster
Wasps v Toulouse
Cardiff v Milan
European Conference all pools
Courage Leagues 1,2,3,4N,4S
SRU Tennents Nat Leagues 1/7
Heineken League Divs 2/5
Tue, 29th — Heineken League Div 2
Wed, 30th — Scotland 'A' v Australia

NOVEMBER 1996

Sat, 2nd — Combined Scottish Districts
  v Australia
Heineken Cup (Europe):
  Dax v Pontypridd
  Benetton Treviso v Bath
  Leicester v Llanelli
  Leinster v Pau
  Harlequins v North & Midlands
  Ulster v Brive
  Toulouse v Munster
  Milan v Wasps
European Conference all pools
Pilkington Cup 3rd Round
Courage League 2
Heineken League Divs 2/5
Sun, 3rd — SRU Tennents 1556 Cup Round 2
Tue, 5th — Scottish District Select v Australia
Fri, 8th — Scotland 'A' v Junior Springboks
Sat, 9th — SCOTLAND v AUSTRALIA
IRELAND v Overseas Country
Courage Leagues 1,2,3,4N,4S
Heineken League Divs 1/5
Sun, 10th — SRU Tennents Nat Leagues 1/7
Scotland Develpoment XV v
  Queensland
Wed, 13th — Leinster v Australia
Sat, 16th — Ulster v Australia
European Cup/Conference
  Semi-finals
Courage Leagues 1,2,3,4N,4S
SRU Tennents Premiership 1/4
SRU Tennents Nat Leagues 1/7
Heineken League Divs 1/5
Sun, 17th — Ireland U21 v New Zealand U21
Wed, 20th — Connacht v Australia
London Counties v Argentina
Northern Counties v Queensland
Western Counties v Junior
  Springboks
Thu, 21st — Dubai International Sevens
– Fri, 22nd — (RWC Qualifying)

Sat, 23rd	ENGLAND v ITALY
	Munster v Australia
	London Counties v Junior
	Springboks
	Pilkington Cup 4th Round
	SRU Tennents Premiership 1/4
	SRU Tennents Nat Leagues 1/7
	SWALEC CUP 4th Round
Sun, 24th	Midland Counties v Queensland
	Northern Counties v New
	Zealand Barbarians
	Western Counties v Argentina
Tue, 26th	Ireland 'A' v Australia
Wed, 27th	Midland Counties v Argentina
	Northern Counties v Junior
	Springboks
Thurs, 28th	Western Counties v Queensland
Sat, 30th	ENGLAND v NEW ZEALAND
	BARBARIANS
	IRELAND v AUSTRALIA
	SRU Tennents Premiership 1/4
	SRU Tennents Nat Leagues 1/7
	Heineken League Divs 1/5

DECEMBER 1996

Sun, 1st	London Counties v Queensland
	Midland Counties v Junior
	Springboks
	Northern Counties v Argentina
Wed, 4th	Combined Services v Argentina
Sat, 7th	FRANCE v SOUTH AFRICA
	BARBARIANS v AUSTRALIA
	Courage League 1
	SRU Tennents Premiership 1/4
	SRU Tennents Nat Leagues 1/7
	Heineken League Divs 1,3,4,5
	Irish Insurance Corporation
	League Divs 1/4
Tue, 10th	Oxford v Cambridge
	Oxford U21 v Cambridge U21
	Scotland Development XV v
	Queensland
	England 'A' v Argentina
Wed, 11th	England 'A' v Junior Springboks
Fri, 13th	Scotland U21 v Italy U21
Sat, 14th	ENGLAND v ARGENTINA
	SCOTLAND v ITALY
	SWALEC Cup 5th Round
	Irish Insurance Corporation
	League Divs 1/4 (2)
Sun, 15th	WALES v SOUTH AFRICA
Sat, 21st	Courage Leagues 3,4N,4S
	Pilkington Cup 5th Round
	France v Scotland (Schools)
Sun, 22nd	Scottish Inter-Dist Championship:
	Edinburgh v Glasgow
	North & Midlands v South
	SRU Tennents Premiership 1/4
	Heineken League Divs 1/5
	Irish Insurance Corporation
	League Divs 1/4
Fri, 27th	Leicester v Barbarians

Sat, 28th	Courage Leagues 1,2,3,4N,4S
	Heineken League Divs 1/5
Sun, 29th	Scottish Inter-Dist Championship:
	Glasgow v South
	North & Midlands v Edinburgh

JANUARY 1997

Sat, 4th	IRELAND v ITALY
	European Cup/Conference Finals
	Courage Leagues 1,2,3,4N,4S
	Heineken League Divs 1/5
	Scotland v Wales (Schools)
Sun, 5th	Scottish Inter-Dist Championship:
	Glasgow v North & Midlands
	South v Edinburgh
Sat, 11th	Courage Leagues 1,2,3,4N,4S
	SRU Tennents Premiership 2/4
	SRU Tennents Nat Leagues 1/7
	Heineken League Divs 2/5
	Irish Insurance Corporation
	League Divs 1/4
Fri, 17th	Scotland 'A' v Wales 'A'
	Scotland U21 v Wales U21
Sat, 18th	IRELAND v FRANCE
	SCOTLAND v WALES
	Courage Leagues 1,2,3
Sun, 19th	SRU Tennents 1556 Cup Round 3
Wed, 22nd	Irish Ins Corp League Div 2
	Wanderers v Clontarf
Sat, 25th	Pilkington Cup 6th Round
	Courage Leagues 3,4N,4S
	SRU Tennents Premiership 2/3
	SRU Tennents Nat Leagues 1/7
	SWALEC Cup 6th Round
	Irish Insurance Corporation
	League Divs 1/4
Tue, 28th	Scotland Development XV v
	Otago
Wed, 29th	Irish Ins Corp League Div 2
	Wanderers v DLSP
Fri, 31st	England 'A' v Scotland 'A'
	England U21 v Scotland U21
	England 'A' v Otago
	Wales 'A' v Ireland 'A'
	Wales U21 v Ireland U21

FEBRUARY 1997

Sat, 1st	ENGLAND v SCOTLAND
	WALES v IRELAND
	Courage Leagues 3,4N,4S
Sat, 8th	Courage Leagues 1,2,3,4N,4S
	SRU Tennents Premiership 1/4
	SRU Tennents Nat Leagues 1/7
	Heineken League Divs 1/5
	Irish Insurance Corporation
	League Divs 1/4
Fri, 14th	France 'A' v Wales 'A'
	France U21 v Wales U21
	France v Wales (Students)
	Ireland 'A' v England 'A'
	Ireland U21 v England U21
Sat, 15th	IRELAND v ENGLAND

	FRANCE v WALES
	Courage Leagues 3,4N,4S
	SRU Tennents Premiership 1/4
	SRU Tennents Nat Leagues 1/7
Sat, 22nd	Pilkington Cup Quarter-finals
	Courage Leagues 3,4N,4S
	SRU Tennents Nat Leagues 1/7
	SWALEC Cup 7th Round
	Irish Insurance Corporation League Divs 1/4
Thurs, 27th	England 'A' v France 'A'
Fri, 28th	Scotland 'A' v Ireland 'A'
	Scotland U21 v Ireland U21
	England Colts v Italy Juniors

MARCH 1997

Sat, 1st	ENGLAND v FRANCE
	SCOTLAND v IRELAND
	Courage Leagues 3,4N,4S
	Heineken League Divs 1,3,4,5
Wed, 5th	East Midlands v Barbarians
Sat, 8th	Courage Leagues 2,3,4N,4S
	Scotland U19 v England U19
	SRU Tennents Nat Leagues 1/7
	Heineken League Divs 1/5
	Irish Insurance Corporation Leagues Divs 1/4
Thu, 13th	Scotland U21 v Japan Schools
Fri, 14th	France 'A' v Scotland 'A'
	France U21 v Scotland U21
	Wales v England (Students)
Sat, 15th	FRANCE v SCOTLAND
	WALES v ENGLAND
	Courage Leagues 3,4,N,4S
	Irish Insurance Corporation Leagues Divs 1/4
Wed, 19th	BUSA Final
Fri, 21st to	Cathay Pacific-Hong Kong Bank
Sun, 23rd	Sevens (RWC Sevens)
Sat, 22nd	Courage Leagues 1,2,3,4N,4S
	England 18G v France 18G
	Daily Mail Schools Day
	SWALEC CUP 7th Round
	SRU Tennents 1556 Cup Round 4
	Ireland Insurance Corporation Leagues Divs 1/4
	Heineken League Div 5
Sun, 23rd – Sun, 30th	FIRA Junior World Championships
Sat, 29th	Pilkington Cup semi-finals
	Courage League 1
	Cardiff v Barbarians
	Heineken League Divs 1,3,4
	Irish Insurance Corporation Leagues Divs 1/3
	Ireland 18G v England 18G

APRIL 1997

Wed, 2nd	England 18G v Scotland 18G
Sat, 5th	Courage Leagues 1,2,3,4N,4S
	Heineken League Divs 1,5
	Irish Insurance Corporation Leagues Divs 1 & 2

	Scotland U18 v Ireland U18
Sun, 6th	SRU Tennents 1556 Cup Round 5
Tue, 8th	England v Scotland (Schools)
Sat, 12th	Royal Navy v Army
	Combined Services U21 v England Students U21
	Courage Leagues 1,2,3,4N,4S
	SWALEC Cup Semi-finals
	Irish Insurance Corporation Leagues Divs 1 & 2
	Wales 18G v England 18G
	England Colts v Wales Youth
	Scotland v Ireland (Schools)
Wed, 16th	Army v Royal Air Force
Sat, 19th	County Championship Finals
	Courage Leagues 1,2,3,4N,4S
	Heineken League Divs 1/5
	Wales U19 v Scotland U19
	Wales U18 v Scotland U18
	France Juniors v England Colts
Sun, 20th	SRU Tennents 1556 Cup Quarter-finals
Wed, 23rd	Royal Navy v Royal Air Force
	SRU Youth Leagues Final
Sat, 26th	Courage Leagues 1,2,3,4N,4S
	Heineken League Div 1
Sun, 27th	SRU Tennents 1556 Cup Semi-finals

MAY 1997

Sat, 3rd	Courage Leagues 1,3
	Intermediate & Shield Finals
	Heineken League Div 1
Sat, 10th	Pilkington Cup Final
	SWALEC Cup Final
	SRU Tennents 1556 Cup Finals
Sat, 17th	Middlesex Seven-a-Side Finals
Sat, 24th	Eastern Province Invitation v British Isles
	The Sanyo Cup
Wed, 28th	Western Province v British Isles
Sat, 31st	Orange Free State v British Isles

JUNE 1997

Wed, 4th	Transvaal v British Isles
Sat, 7th	Northern Transvaal v British Isles
Wed, 11th	South Eastern Transvaal v British Isles
Sat, 14th	Natal v British Isles
Tue, 17th	Emerging Springboks v British Isles
Sat, 21st	SOUTH AFRICA v BRITISH ISLES (1st Test)
Tue, 24th	Border v British Isles
Sat, 28th	SOUTH AFRICA v BRITISH ISLES (2nd Test)

JULY 1997

| Tue, 1st | South African Barbarians v British Isles |
| Sat, 5th | SOUTH AFRICA v BRITISH ISLES (3rd Test) |

REVIEW

Wooden Spoon Society

A SUMMARY OF THE SEASON

BY **BILL MITCHELL**

INTERNATIONAL RUGBY

WALES IN SOUTH AFRICA
AUGUST 1995

Opponents	Results	
S.E. Transvaal	L	6 –47
SOUTH AFRICA	L	11 –40

Played 2 Lost 2

ENGLAND COLTS IN CANADA
AUGUST-SEPTEMBER 1995

Opponents	Results	
Y. Newfoundland	W	37 – 6
Ontario U-21	W	19 –16
Ontario U-19	W	60 – 6
Alberta U-21	W	72 – 9
B.Columbia U-20	W	58 – 0
YOUNG CANADA	W	15 –12

Played 6 Won 6

NEW ZEALAND IN ITALY & FRANCE
OCTOBER-NOVEMBER 1995

Opponents	Results	
Italy 'A'	W	51 –21
ITALY	W	70 – 6
French Babrarians	W	34 –19
Languedoc-Rouss.	W	30 – 9
Basque Landes	W	47 –20
FRANCE	L	15 –22
French Selection	W	55 –17
FRANCE	W	37 –12

Played 8 Won 7 Lost 1

FIJI IN WALES & IRELAND
OCTOBER-NOVEMBER 1995

Opponents	Results	
Wales 'A'	W	25 –10
Neath	L	22 –30
Cardiff	L	21 –22
Treorchy	W	70 –14
Pontypridd	L	13 –31
Llanelli	W	38 –12
WALES	L	15 –19
Connacht	L	5 –27
IRELAND	L	8 –44

Played 9 Won 3 Lost 6

WESTERN SAMOA IN SCOTLAND
& ENGLAND
NOVEMBER-DECEMBER 1995

Opponents	Results	
Edinburgh	W	35 –22
Scotland 'A'	W	27 – 9
Scot N & Mid	L	9 –43
SCOTLAND	D	15 –15
Cambridge U.	L	14 –22
London Division	W	40 –32
Midland Division	L	19 –40
North Division	L	8 –34
South W. Division	W	31 –16
England 'A'	L	0 –55
ENGLAND	L	9 –27

Played 12 Won 5 Drawn 1 Lost 6

TRANSVAAL IN BRITISH ISLES
NOVEMBER-DECEMBER 1995

Opponents	Results
Leicester	L 14 – 39
Bristol	W 26 – 12
Leinster	L 6 – 15
Newcastle	W 38 – 13
Munster	D 16 – 16

Played 5 Won 2 Drawn 1 Lost 2

NEW SOUTH WALES IN BRITISH ISLES
JANUARY-FEBRUARY 1996

Opponents	Results
Bristol	W 34 – 23
Newport	W 24 – 16
Pontypridd	cancelled
England 'A'	L 22 – 24
Leinster	W 33 – 19
Ulster	L 33 – 40
Scottish Dev. XV	W 40 – 11
Newcastle	W 30 – 21
Coventry	W 27 – 26

Played 8 Won 6 Lost 2 Cancelled 1

SCOTLAND IN NEW ZEALAND
MAY-JUNE 1996

Opponents	Results
Wanganui	W 49 – 13
Northland	L 10 – 15
Waikato	L 35 – 39
Southland	W 31 – 21
South Island XV	W 63 – 21
NEW ZEALAND	L 31 – 62
Bay of Plenty	W 35 – 21
NEW ZEALAND	L 12 – 36

Played 8 Won 4 Lost 4

WALES IN AUSTRALIA
MAY-JUNE 1996

Opponents	Results
Western Australia	W 62 – 20
A.C.T.	L 30 – 69
New South Wales	L 20 – 27
AUSTRALIA	L 25 – 56
Australia 'B'	L 41 – 51
N.S.W. Country	W 49 – 3
Victoria	W 42 – 9
AUSTRALIA	L 3 – 42

Played 8 Won 3 Lost 5

CANADA IN AUSTRALIA
JUNE 1996

Opponents	Results
Queensland 'A'	L 6 – 23
New South Wales	L 19 – 44
South Australia	W 19 – 13
Australian U.	W 19 – 6
\AUSTRALIA	L 9 – 74

Played 5 Won 2 Lost 3

FRANCE IN ARGENTINA
JUNE 1996

Opponents	Results
B. Aires Seleccion	L 26 – 29
Tucuman Seleccion	W 20 – 10
ARGENTINA	W 34 – 27
San Juan Seleccion	W 51 – 0
ARGENTINA	W 34 – 15

Played 5 Won 4 Lost 1

THE FIVE NATIONS CHAMPIONSHIP 1996

Results

France	15	England	12
Ireland	10	Scotland	16
England	21	Wales	15
Scotland	19	France	14
France	45	Ireland	10
Wales	14	Scotland	16
Ireland	30	Wales	17
Scotland	9	England	18
England	28	Ireland	15
Wales	16	France	15

	P	W	L	F	A	Trs	Pts
England	4	3	1	79	54	3	6
Scotland	4	3	1	60	56	5	6
France	4	2	2	89	57	10	4
Wales	4	1	3	62	82	6	2
Ireland	4	1	3	65	106	6	2

TRI-NATIONS TOURNAMENT 1996

New Zealand	43	Australia	6
Australia	21	South Africa	16
New Zealand	52	South Africa	12
Australia	25	New Zealand	22
South Africa	26	Australia	19
South Africa	18	New Zealand	29

	P	W	D	L	F	A	Pts
New Zealand	4	4	0	0	119	60	17
South Africa	4	1	0	3	73	84	6
Australia	4	1	0	3	71	116	6

OTHER INTERNATIONAL MATCHES 1995–96

FULL INTERNATIONAL RESULTS

Canam match

Canada	14	U.S.A.	15

Latin Cup

France	34	Italy	22
Argentina	51	Romania	16
France	52	Romania	8
Argentina	26	Italy	6
Argentina	12	France	47
Italy	40	Romania	3

	P	W	L	F	A	Pts
France	3	3	0	133	42	6
Argentina	3	2	1	89	69	4
Italy	3	1	2	68	53	2
Romania	3	0	3	27	143	0

Italy	21	S. Africa	40
England	14	S. Africa	24
U.S.A.	18	Ireland	25
Wales	31	Italy	26
France	64	Romania	12
S. Africa	43	Fiji	18

'A' and UNDER-21 MATCHES 1995-96

England U-21	21	Scotland U-21	18
Italy A	29	Scotland A	18
Italy U21	10	Scotland U-21	31
Ireland A	26	Scotland A	19
France A	15	England A	25
Ireland U-21	21	Scotland U-21	9
Scotland U-21	3	France U-21	29
Scotland A	38	France A	32
Wales U-21	25	Scotland U-21	21
Wales A	22	Scotland A	32
Ireland A	25	Wales A	11
Ireland U-21	20	Wales U-21	12
Italy A	19	England A	22
England A	56	Ireland A	26
Wales A	13	France A	34
England U-21	3	France U-21	40
Italy U-21	8	England U-21	39

STUDENT AND UNIVERSITY
MATCHES 1995–96

France Stu.	33	England Stu.	14
England Stu.	31	Wales Stu.	19
England Univs	8	Wales Univs	38
Scotland Stu.	9	England Stu.	44
Scotland Univs	10	England Univs	34
England Stu.	19	Ireland Stu.	24
Wales Stu.	15	France Stu.	41
Scotland Stu.	26	France Stu.	33
N.Z. Stu.	28	England Stu.	23

STUDENTS WORLD CUP

Quarter-finals

France	38	New Zealand	29
Argentina	46	Italy	12
South Africa	30	Wales	25
Scotland	71	Japan	47

Semi-finals

France	31	Argentina	19
South Africa	53	Scotland	31

Third place play-off

Argentina	42	Scotland	19

Final

France	38	South Africa	19

WORLD YOUTH CHAMPIONSHIP

Semi-finals

Wales	21	Romania	16
Argentina	41	Scotland	20

Third place play-off

Romania	32	Scotland	6

Final

Argentina	34	Wales	7

CATHAY PACIFIC-
HONGKONG BANK SEVENS

Cup Final

New Zealand	19	Fiji	17

Plate Final

France	45	Hong Kong	12

Bowl Final

Japan	55	Namibia	21

WOMEN'S RUGBY 1995-96

Home Internationals
Results

Ireland	3	Scotland	21
England	56	Wales	3
Wales	11	Scotland	6
Ireland	6	Wales	22
Scotland	8	England	12
England	43	Ireland	8

	P	W	L	F	A	Pts
England	3	3	0	111	19	6
Wales	3	2	1	36	68	4
Scotland	3	1	2	35	26	2
Ireland	3	0	3	17	86	0

Other international

France	6	England	15

CLUB, COUNTY AND DIVISIONAL RUGBY

ENGLAND

Pilkington Cup
Quarter-finals

Bristol	12	Bath	19
Gloucester	22	Wasps	9
Leicester	24	Harlequins	9
London Irish	11	W Hartlepool	10

Semi-finals

Bath	19	Gloucester	12
London Irish	21	Leicester	46

Final

Bath	16	Leicester	15

Pilkington Shield Final

Helston	6	Medicals	16

Courage Leagues
Division 1

	P	W	D	L	F	A	Pts
Bath	18	15	1	2	575	276	31
Leicester	18	15	0	3	476	242	30
Harlequins	18	13	0	5	524	314	26
Wasps	18	11	0	7	439	322	22
Sale	18	9	1	8	365	371	19
Bristol	18	8	0	10	329	421	16
Orrell	18	7	0	11	323	477	14
Gloucester	18	6	0	12	275	370	12
Saracens	18	5	0	13	284	451	10
W Hartlepool	18	0	0	18	288	634	0

Division 2

	P	W	D	L	F	A	Pts
North'ton	18	18	0	0	867	203	36
London I.	18	15	0	3	584	405	30
London Sc.	18	10	2	6	361	389	22
Wakefield	18	8	0	10	328	331	16
Waterloo	18	7	2	9	309	483	16
Moseley	18	7	0	11	327	447	14
Blackheath	18	6	1	11	341	469	13
Newcastle	18	5	1	12	348	405	11
Nottingham	18	5	1	12	333	433	11
Bedford	18	5	1	12	287	520	11

Division 3 champions: Coventry
Runners-up: Richmond
Division 4: Exeter

CIS County Championships
Semi-finals

Lancashire	16	Warwickshire	36
Surrey	13	Gloucs	16

Final

Gloucs	17	Warwickshire	13

University Match

Oxford U	19	Cambridge U	21

University Second Teams Match

Oxford U	7	Cambridge U	8

University Under-21 Match

Oxford U	13	Cambridge U	3

British Universities Final

Cardiff Inst	6	Loughboro' U	3

British Universities Women's Final

Birmingham U	5	Loughboro' U	32

Hospitals Cup

St Mary's	26	Charing X-Westminster	22

Sanyo Cup

Leicester	31	World XV	40

Inter-Services Champions: Triple tie
Securicor Trophy: British Police
Middlesex 7s Winners: Wigan RLFC
Shell UK Ltd -Rosslyn Park Schools Sevens Festival Winners: Bryanston
Open winners: Stonyhurst
Sybase London Sevens Winners: Wasps

Women's National Cup Final

Richmond	17	Saracens	35

Women's Students' National Cup Final

Loughbro' U	7	Brunel U	17

Inter-code matches
(RL Rules)

Wigan	82	Bath	6

(RU Laws)

Bath	44	Wigan	19

WALES

SWALEC Welsh Challenge Cup
Quarter-finals

Llanelli	11	Cardiff	10
Neath	44	Dunvant	11
Newbridge	15	Pontypridd	20
Newport	16	Caerhilly	10

Semi-finals

Llanelli	17	Pontypridd	31
Neath	24	Newport	22

Final

Neath	22	Pontypridd	29

Division 1

	P	W	D	L	T	B	Pts
Neath	22	17	1	4	121	37	72
Cardiff	22	18	1	3	119	35	72
Pontypridd	22	16	1	5	98	28	61
Llanelli	22	15	0	7	88	29	59
Bridgend	22	12	1	9	73	22	47
Swansea	22	11	0	11	83	22	44
Ebbw Vale	22	11	0	11	44	8	30
Newport	22	10	1	11	43	9	30
Newbridge	22	9	0	13	47	11	29
Treorchy	22	5	1	16	45	10	21
Aberavon	22	3	0	19	38	8	14
Abertillery	22	2	0	20	43	8	14

Division 2

	P	W	D	L	T	B	Pts
Dunvant	22	18	0	5	73	22	56
Caerphilly	22	18	0	4	57	14	50
Cross Keys	22	11	0	11	68	18	40
Pontypool	22	12	0	10	63	15	39
Bonymaen	22	10	0	12	55	14	34
Llandovery	22	11	2	9	37	5	29
Maesteg	22	10	1	11	38	7	28
Abercynon	22	10	0	12	39	6	26
Ystr'lais	22	10	1	11	38	5	26
S W. Police	22	7	0	15	49	11	25
Llanharan	22	9	0	13	41	6	24
Tenby Utd.	22	4	0	18	33	4	12

Division 3 champions: Blackwood
Runners-up: Cardiff Institute
Division 4 champions: Merthyr
Runners-up: Rumney

SCOTLAND

Tennnets Inter-District Championship

	P	W	D	L	F	A	Pts
Exiles	4	4	0	0	100	50	8
Edinburgh	4	2	0	2	109	82	4
Nth & Mid	4	2	0	2	95	72	4
Sth of Scot	4	2	0	2	80	82	4
Glasgow	4	0	0	4	63	161	0

Tennents 1556 Cup Final

Hawick	17	Watsonians	15

Tennents 1556 Shield Final

Currie	75	Stirling Co.	20

Tennents 1556 Bowl Final

Edinburgh A	28	Selkirk	21

McEwan's National Leagues
Division 1

	P	W	D	L	F	A	Pts
Melrose	14	9	1	4	326	199	19
Stirling C.	14	9	1	4	321	215	19
Watsonians	14	8	1	5	393	270	17
Boro'muir	14	7	2	5	327	302	16
Hawick	14	7	0	7	243	288	14
Heriot's FP	13	5	1	7	278	360	11
E'burgh A	14	4	1	9	243	282	9
Gala	13	2	1	10	179	394	5

Division 2

	P	W	D	L	F	A	Pts
Currie	14	11	0	3	357	266	22
Jed-Forest	14	10	0	4	302	185	20
Glasgow H	14	8	0	6	375	239	16
W. of Scot.	14	7	0	7	268	258	14
Dundee HS	14	6	0	8	259	239	12
Kelso	14	6	0	8	275	260	12
Selkirk	14	6	0	8	215	307	10
S.Melville FP	14	3	0	11	193	490	6

Division 3 champions: Glasgow A.
Runners-up: Biggar
Division 4 champions: Kilmarnock
Runners-up: Glasgow Southern

IRELAND

Insurance Corporation All-Ireland League

Division 1

	P	W	D	L	F	A	Pts
Shannon	10	8	0	2	156	78	16
Garryowen	10	8	0	2	171	165	16
Cork Const	10	7	0	3	208	149	14
Y. Munster	10	7	0	3	208	149	14
St Mary's	10	5	1	4	147	119	11
Lansdowne	10	4	1	5	180	172	9
Ballymena	10	4	1	5	157	181	9
Old Wesley	10	3	1	6	156	164	7
Blackrock	10	3	0	7	160	208	6
O. B'vedere	10	3	0	7	135	189	6
Instonians	10	1	0	9	145	233	2

Division 2

	P	W	D	L	F	A	Pts
O. Crescent	10	9	1	0	246	103	19
Dungannon	10	7	1	2	254	171	15
Terenure	10	7	1	2	191	118	15
Bective R.	10	6	0	4	186	104	12
Greystones	10	5	1	4	164	173	11
Sunday's W	10	4	2	4	223	194	10
Malone	10	5	0	5	205	220	10
Wanderers	10	4	0	6	167	206	8
Clontarf	10	3	0	7	130	212	6
Dolphin	10	1	0	9	165	245	2
N of Ireland	10	1	0	9	157	299	2

Inter-Provincial Championship

	P	W	D	L	F	A	Pts
Leinster	4	4	0	0	133	53	8
Ulster	4	3	0	1	73	53	6
Munster	4	2	0	2	84	50	4
Exiles	4	1	0	3	71	113	2
Connacht	4	0	0	4	43	135	0

Senior Provincial Cup winners:

Connacht:	Galwegians
Leinster:	Terenure College
Munster:	Shannon
Ulster:	Dungannon

FRANCE

French Club Championship

Semi-finals

Brive	23	Pau	19
Toulouse	36	Dax	23

Final

Toulouse	20	Brive	13

ITALY

Cup Final

Milan	23	Treviso	19

NEW ZEALAND

Championship First Division 1995

Semi-finals

Counties	32	Otago	41
Auckland	60	N. Harbour	26

Final

Auckland	23	Otago	19

Ranfurly Shield Holders: Auckland

SOUTH AFRICA

Currie Cup Final 1995

Natal	25	W. Province	17

INTERNATIONAL CLUB/REPRESENTATIVE RUGBY

BARBARIAN FC

Opponents		Results
Stirling County	W	57 – 34
Newport	W	59 – 28
Leicester	L	25 – 51
East Midlands	L	19 – 47
Cardiff	L	43 – 49
IRELAND	W	70 – 38
Kansai Pres. XV	L	66 – 76
Kobe Steel	L	43 – 63

Played 8 Won 3 Lost 5

HEINEKEN EUROPEAN CUP

POOL A

F. Constanta	10	Toulouse	54
Treviso	86	F. Constanta	8
Toulouse	18	Treviso	9

Final Table

	P	W	D	L	F	A	Pts
Toulouse	2	2	0	0	72	19	4
Treviso	2	1	0	1	95	26	2
F.Constanta	2	0	0	2	18	140	0

POOL B

Bordeaux	14	Cardiff	14
Cardiff	46	Ulster	6
Ulster	16	Bordeaux	29

Final Table

	P	W	D	L	F	A	Pts
Cardiff	2	1	1	0	60	20	3
Bordeaux	2	1	1	0	43	30	3
Ulster	2	0	0	2	22	75	0

POOL C

Milan	21	Leinster	24
Pontypridd	31	Milan	12
Leinster	23	Pontypridd	22

Final Table

	P	W	D	L	F	A	Pts
Leinster	2	2	0	0	47	43	4
Pontypridd	2	1	0	1	53	35	2
Milan	2	0	0	2	33	55	0

POOL D

Munster	17	Swansea	13
Castres	19	Munster	12
Swansea	22	Castres	10

Final Table

	P	W	D	L	F	A	Pts
Swansea	2	1	0	1	35	27	2
Munster	2	1	0	1	29	32	2
Castres	2	1	0	1	29	34	2

Semi-finals

Leinster	14	Cardiff	23
Toulouse	30	Swansea	3

Final

Cardiff	18	Toulouse	21

SUPER 12 TOURNAMENT

Final Table

	P	W	D	L	F	A	Pts
Queensland	11	9	0	2	320	247	41
Auckland	11	8	0	3	408	354	41
N.Transvaal	11	8	0	3	329	208	38
Natal	11	6	0	5	389	277	33
A.C.T.	11	7	0	4	306	273	32
Waikato	11	6	0	5	291	269	28
N.S.W.	11	5	0	6	312	290	28
Otago	11	5	0	6	332	391	26
Wellington	11	3	0	8	290	356	17
Transvaal	11	3	0	8	233	299	16
W. Province	11	3	1	7	252	353	15
Canterbury	11	2	1	8	234	378	13

Semi-finals

Queensland	25	Natal	43
Auckland	48	N. Transvaal	11

Final

Auckland	45	Natal	21